How call backs kill your business!

**JASON BLEVINS
PETER LISOSKIE**

How call backs kill your business

© 2016 Jason Blevins & Peter Lisoskie

All rights reserved. No portion of this book may be produced, stored in a retrieval system, or transmitted in any form or by any means—electronic, mechanical, photocopy, recording, scanning, or other, - except for brief quotations in critical reviews or articles, without prior written permission of the publisher.

Limit of Liability/Disclaimer of Warranty: While the publisher and author used their best efforts in preparing this book, they make no representations or warranties regarding the accuracy or completeness of the contents of this book. The publisher and author specifically disclaim any implied warranties or merchantability or fitness for a particular purpose, and make no guarantees whatsoever that you will achieve any particular result. Any case studies that are presented herein do not necessarily represent what you would expect to achieve, since business success depends on a variety of factors. We believe all case studies and results presented herein are true and accurate, but we have not audited the results. The advice and strategies contained in this book may not even be suitable for your situation, and you should consult your own advisors as appropriate. The publisher and the author shall not be held liable for any loss of profit or any other commercial damages, including but not limited to special, incidental, consequential, or other damages. The fact that an organization or website is referred to in this work as a citation and/or a potential source of information does not mean that the publisher or author endorses the information the organization or website may provide or the recommendations it may make. Further, readers should be aware that internet websites listed in this work may have changed or disappeared after this work was written.

The One Day Close Coaching Group can bring these authors to your live event. For more information or to book an event visit The One Day Close Coaching Group at **www.theonedayclose.com.**

Book created, developed, marketed, and launched using processes, tools, and technologies of:

ISBN-13: 978-1517205850

www.inviralacademy.com

Dedication

Jason's Dedication….

To my wife who has an unparalleled drive and work ethic in life. She is my companion and best friend. She has been with me through my trials and errors and ups and downs as a salesman. She has been a strong supporter through all my struggles and my biggest cheerleader through my eventual successes. I'm often amazed at how she can be an irreplaceable employee at her own career and hold down the fort with four kids when I'm gone.

To my kids for their sacrifices when I was gone as I traveled to make a living, compiled content and learned to perfect my craft. It has not been easy but sometimes we need to take the road less traveled. I hope it serves as a lesson to work hard and always chase your passions.

I love you all.

Peter's Dedication….

To my father who taught me about work ethic, creativity, and character.

To my mother who helped me understand the power of empathy and compassion in everything I do.

To my siblings who helped me learn the importance of sharing.

To my first work mentor, Dick Burger who taught me how to be an authentic leader by setting a vision and linking that with everyone on the team.

To Dan Samoza who shared his abilities and insights on what it means to be a great coach.

To my life partner Patricia who is my rock of support and cheerleader in everything I set out to accomplish.

To my sons who teach me how to make an impact and leave a legacy that can be passed from one generation to the next.

Meet Jason Blevins

After ten years in the Navy, Jason entered into the world of sales. He began by representing an industry leading insurance company out of Virginia. In just nine months, he opened up more business than anyone in the state. He scooped up all the corporate sponsored trips and cash bonuses offered. Following his first year with the company, he was quickly promoted into a management role where he had his first taste of trying to train others to do what he does. Being dissatisfied with caring more for his team's success than they did, it was time for a change.

Jason sold insurance to a remodeling company that saw his potential. They offered him a job as an in home sale rep. Looking for a new challenge, he accepted the offer. In the 22 years this company was in business, not one sale rep ever eclipsed 1 million in sales. Hired at the end of March, Jason was the first as he passed 1.4 million in just nine months. Naturally, the owner asked Jason to help him open a satellite office and again train others to do what he did. This was his second time faced with this challenge and again, just like before, it was time for a change.

Next, Jason went on to start his own company. He knew what he was good at and what he was not good at. If he could just stay in front of people and sell, he was happy but the problem was, if he wanted to grow, he was going to have to figure out how to train people to do what he did best. In his own business, he accomplished just that. He pursued mentorship from some of the best in the industry and invested in workshops. He was thriving, even against all odds in a down economy. That is, until he and his wife decided they wanted to move to Pennsylvania to raise their family. He sold his file cabinet and made the move.

Jason moved to an ideal location in Pennsylvania where a position became available as a Territory Manager for one of the top manufacturers of building products. One of the biggest responsibilities is to communicate to his customers how to promote his products. Being told time and time again how valuable his selling practices were, it became more and more obvious that he needed to share his processes with the masses.

How call backs kill your business!

Meet Peter Lisoskie

I was taught by a sales mentor long ago two key ingredients to selling. First, you can't sell anything to anybody. You can only create a discovery process for them to buy. Second, affordability is tied to belief. If they believe in your product, your price, and they believe in you, with everything else being equal, they can afford what you have to offer.

Growing up, Pete learned a hard work ethic from his father, teamwork from playing sports, and selling lessons from his grandfather.

After attending college, he started his first engineering job where he met his most influential mentor Dick Burger who was his first boss. Dick helped him understand the power of inspiring people through communication, empathy, authenticity which he adapted in his selling style.

Pete used Dick's teachings to create his own journey and rapidly advanced in working and leading product development divisions in payment transaction, consumer goods, medical, bioscience, and bio-tech industries. He quickly became known and recruited as the 'turn-around' expert for companies. What he found by helping these companies, is the success or failure of any situation was all about inspiring people towards a powerful vision and mission.

Over the last 15 years, Pete started and built a home services company with $15,000 in his pocket to a $5.2 million dollar revenue producer using the same techniques that he and Jason talk about in this book. His belief was the best sale is one that happens before you leave on the first visit and he taught this to his General Managers who used these teachings to create jobs for the team without having to do countless follow up calls.

Pete developed the One Day Close book and program with his partner Jason Blevins to help teach others the same system that works. In the book, Pete shares his experience, knowledge, and passion for selling through stories and viewpoints on the key elements of what he believes it takes to become an effective sales professional. One that gives the owner of the company peace of mind as they know they'll not only get the job but will foster relationships in any neighborhood to create new work through using our system.

One Day Workshops & Online Courses

As the owner of a remodeling business, have you ever wondered...
- Why is it so hard to find good salespeople?
- How do I retain good salespeople?
- How do I get out of working in my business to working on my business?
- How can I increase my sales numbers through my team?
- How can I get my team's closing ratio up?
- Is there a process that can be duplicated?
- How can I get my sales team to get the deal on the first visit?
- How can I get an edge over my competition?
- How can my team pick up some leads on their own?

What if you could...
- Hire and keep good salespeople
- Free time up for yourself and put energy into your business
- Put more money towards your bottom line
- Get a greater return on investment with your marketing dollars
- Strike fear in the hearts of your competition!

Remember when selling in the home used to be fun? What happened? Why are business owners working so hard just to keep the lights on? The One Day Close was created, field tested and mastered to bring back a selling process that has been lost over the years of a down economy. It's time to make money at this thing again. In fact, it's time your company has a break-out year. With The One Day Close system, you can do just that.

www.theonedayclose.com   (717)292-8686

Table of Contents

Introduction:	**Why Read this book?**	**8**
Chapter 1:	**Appointment Setting/ Gaining Trust**	**10**
Chapter 2:	**The Process**	**65**
Chapter 3:	**The Close**	**79**
Chapter 4:	**Tips and Techniques**	**96**

Introduction Why Read This Book?

When I was an in-home salesperson, I was happy. I would generally have maybe two appointments a day through the week and maybe one on a Saturday. I had plenty of time to work out, do things around the house and run errands. My life was mindlessly easy and I made a lot of money because I was good at sales.

I saw plenty of people around me that struggled. It was downright painful to witness my peers failing. We would have our weekly meetings and "touch" on some sales techniques. I was grateful that I was rarely the reason why my boss would lose his temper and display his obvious frustrations with the sales team and their lack of performance.

I decided to start my own business. I had a grand plan and in my mind, I could not fail. It didn't take long for me to realize the same dissatisfaction my old boss was feeling. It was infinitely frustrating. I would think to myself, "Why am I allowing my sales staff to plow through my expensive leads with little results?" I would also think, "Why is it so hard to find good sales people?" Like all business owners, I would walk my people through the failed sale from the night before in an attempt to find out where the breakdown was while it was still fresh in their minds. Sometimes this worked but usually, I was just left feeling like I wasn't getting the whole story. Then it hit me like a ton of bricks. I need to spend more time teaching and grooming my people so that my process became so embedded in their minds, that it was as if I was right there on their shoulder in the home.

The problem is, most owners simply don't have the time it takes to train each salesperson the way they want. Most owners default to promoting their best sales representative to sales manager. Now, the owner pays that sales manager more money while the sales manager spends too much time trying to teach everyone else rather than doing what he does best, which is selling in the home. The owner gets super frustrated because he sees the financials. Why is this plan not working?

This is my message to you owners. STOP WASTING MONEY ON THINGS THAT DON'T WORK! Get back to working on your business instead of in your business. From your perspective, you should only spend money on things that yield an ROI (return on investment). You paid for precious leads and your sales reps are devastating them with call-backs. "The One Day Close" is designed to be a hyper focused opportunity for your sales staff to quickly get to the root of what does and does not work in the home. By taking the time to dive into my program, you will not only gain a distinct and competitive advantage over your competition but your business will once again thrive and that is something truly invaluable.

Chapter 1: Appointment Setting/Gaining Trust

"Appointment Setting/Gaining Trust" is going to take you through all the little details that make a significant impact on the end user and their first impression of you. There is so much power in this stage that some would consider this the most important piece of the sales process. This first chapter brings clarity to the point that the salesperson is part of the product. This chapter explores how to dial in on your audience, how to dress for your appointment, and all the little details that make the right first impression.

Peter: I'm Peter Lisoskie, and we are here with Jason Blevins. Jason, how are you doing?

Jason: Fantastic! How are you?

Peter: I'm doing good. Jason, we know your name. Tell us a little bit about what you do.

Jason: I go out into the market and deal with contractors to teach them how to promote their products in the remodeling world to the end user.

Peter: So this product is really for salespeople, is that correct? For people who are out actually doing the selling?

Jason: Correct. Generally catering to a professional sales force for medium to large-sized companies that deal with windows, roofing, siding in the remodeling world.

Peter: That was kind of your background with the windows, siding and working-type situations?

Jason: Correct. I went into a company a decade ago, and started in-home sales. I made a lot of money and started my own Company, like good salespeople generally do. Then they get out. They realize they're pretty good at this thing, so they hire people and train them. It's a fun business and I'll tell you, once you get into this world, you don't get out.

The whole reason I do this is to teach people if you're not going to get out of this thing, then why not just be the best at it and perfect your craft?

Peter: Along that line, for someone reading this book or doing your workshop, what is the big opportunity for them? It seems like there's a lot of this kind of stuff out there already, so why did you decide to produce this product at this time?

Jason: Nothing really other than the fact I've had enough feedback where people say, "Hey, you should write a book. You should put all your thoughts and processes out there, because it's very helpful." So why not? I figured I could reach the masses in a bigger way here.

I think there's been kind of a disconnect, if you will, in the market for years. It's been so price-driven that sales process has kind of been lost. I'm not reinventing the wheel here, but that sales process has been lost.

The days of walking around, measuring your house, "Here's your price – give me a call when you're ready," that's kind of over. There's nothing more maddening to the owner of a company like that when their salespeople quite frankly don't know what they're doing in the home.

I want to kind of reel it all back in and give that distinct advantage to those folks who really do want to increase their sales activity and bring a paycheck home to their family.

Peter: Just adding to that, like you I was in the home services industry for years, and I've got a radio show where we talk about that called Home Matters. I interview a lot of people who have large companies, and I really agree with you that it's time the sales professional comes back.

Even the word "contractor" has gotten a bad reputation and a bad name. It's really representative of the people who are in the client's home, and then how the company deals with the people all the way through the process. So I'm glad you're doing this and really raising the bar for sales professionalism out there, because they're the first into the home. You're exactly right.

So the big opportunity is they should be reading this or taking your video course just because it really will help them. There are probably a lot of people out there too, I would imagine, who are in sales that aren't getting the results they want. They're not getting the conversions or commissions they want.

They're scratching their head. They see other people like them who are successful, and they're probably wondering, *what are they doing that I'm not?*

Jason: That's correct. You're spot on with that for sure. I've seen it. I've been a part of sales organizations where you have the guys on the bottom becoming discouraged. They want to ride with you and figure out what you're doing. They're willing to sacrifice lead time to go into the field with you and figure it out. And then when they come back they're like, "Well, I don't really know what's different about what you did."

The reality is it's all the little things you need to pay attention to that add up to get you closer to that sale.

Peter: We're going to talk about that today. So we're going to "dive" into Jason's brain, so to speak, to understand the process he goes through. What are all these little things he picks up that complete the whole process that transcends you from just a regular sales jockey, to a sales professional?

I've got to ask you, Jason, because this always comes up just like everybody asks about price. One of the things I want to know is why should we listen to Jason Blevins? What's your background? What's your story?

Jason: I did ten years in the Navy. I got out in 2003, and was an air traffic controller. I got out to be an air traffic controller, because if I stayed in and retired I would be too old for the FAA, so it just didn't make sense. I had to make a decision.

So halfway to the ten-year mark I decided to get out. I tried to be a controller. Where I wanted to control traffic they stopped hiring, so I didn't have any options. So I threw my resume out there, and got picked up by a well-known insurance company that's been around for over 60+ years.

I started in March, and by the end of the year, I opened more accounts than anybody else in the entire state I was in. I got recognized and lifted the eyebrows in corporate because I opened so many accounts. I went on all the trips. Went to Puerto Rico and got all the cash bonuses. The state coordinator called me in to meet with all the higher-ups and all the management. They had to know what the heck I was doing.

Back then I didn't realize there was some uniqueness there, and that I might have the ability to sell and connect with people in a way others just didn't. They were going through the motions, and were kind of neglecting some of the body language and things that to me are trivial and make sense. For some people it may be a little more complex than that.

I just absolutely killed it in that business. But what was killing me was wearing the soles off my shoes and knocking on doors. I had enough of that.

So then I moved on after I sold insurance to a remodeling company. They said, "We had five reps from your company come in here before you. But for some reason we're pulling the trigger on you. Would you be interested in a job?"

Peter: The trigger they were pulling was they offered you a job?

Jason: Right. Exactly.

Peter: That's pretty funny.

Jason: They asked me if I would come work for them. And after answering a few questions – one of them being I don't have to go out and procure the business? They were actually providing the leads for me, and all I had to do was go in and sell it. I was in. Sign me up.

I went into that business. That company had been around for 22 years. Again, I came in in March. For some reason March has been my time-frame where I start with all these companies. But for [only] nine months in a company I wrote $1.4 million in business since I started.

Peter: Wow!

Jason: I had never been in the industry before. Nobody in the history of 22 years of that business had ever written over $1 million. Most of the sales reps were writing $600,000 to $700,000, and maybe if they were good $800,000. But no one cleared $1 million – no one got there.

Peter: Hold on for a second. I want to get some clarity on this just to make sure I

How call backs kill your business!

understand. You're saying that all the sales reps over a 22-year period never got to over $1 million within 12 months, and you did it within nine months just starting there.

Jason: That's correct.

Peter: Wow!

Jason: Of course I made 10% commission, so do the math. I was loving it!

Peter: Good paycheck.

Jason: With that I got thrust into a management role. Of course you see something like that from the owner's perspective. He needed to put me in a position where I could train the other folks. And then he gave me a satellite office, and one thing led to another.

Then I realized why am I doing this for 10% when I could be doing it for myself? So I went out and became his competition. I started my own business and had tremendous success with that as well.

The only reason I stopped doing it was because I was in Virginia, and my wife wanted to move back home to Pennsylvania. So I sold my file cabinet, moved up to Pennsylvania, and then I became the manufacturer's rep for the very products I used to sell.

Peter: So you became the competition, which typically happens with guys like you who are really good at what you do. When you had your own business, were you writing north of $1 million as well?

Jason: That's correct. I was doing quite well with that by just about anybody's standards starting a new business. And of course, having to figure out all the logistics.

The thing that made that maybe a little more challenging for me was I couldn't stay in the sales process all the time. I had to hire people, run the business and do all that stuff.

Where a lot of people have struggles when they start their own business is they're either good at sales or they're good at business. But it's hard to find someone who's good at both. That was a bit of a struggle, but I overcame that and had some success with my company.

Peter: It sounds like you're a pretty profits-oriented type of guy. Speaking of that process now, backing up before you pull up in your car, there are some things you feel need to be done as far as the appointment, the follow-ups and things like that. So let's start there, and we'll go all the way through the close step-by-step of each module here.

Why don't you talk to us about the calls that come in and when you're assigned the call? Then what happens as far as confirming appointments, showing up and all that kind of stuff?

Jason: When people call in for an appointment they generally call you from some media source, unless it's word-of-mouth. Then if it's word-of-mouth it's a little more personal than that.

But if they're calling you from a media source (i.e., paper, advertising, pay-per-click or something like that), they're looking for something. But they're looking for something from five other people. So when they call you they're calling other folks.

And it's generally three to five estimates. It got to the point of being ridiculous where homeowners are calling for five estimates it becomes just a matter of price, so that's where I think the disconnect has been happening. People realize it's just about price – they don't care about my sales process. Let me just measure and get my price, and I'll be the low guy.

It kills all the bigger companies that have the overhead. So for bigger companies that have the overhead, offices and sales force, I think this is something that's truly going to help them.

But getting back to the call: So when they call in you're going to set the appointment with them, whatever makes sense. But when you set the appointment you've got to make sure you have both spouses there. If you don't have them both there, you're kind of wasting your time.
It's almost done on purpose on their end. They don't want to close the deal because they want to get through all their other estimates. And then they'll make a decision based on price because everything gets too convoluted.

Peter: Jason, I'm assuming the office person was the one taking the call and setting the appointment for you, correct?

Jason: Right. You'd have an admin person who would take the call. It goes down to the silliness of making sure that when your administrator answers the call they're smiling to give that good first impression. It's like they hear you smiling on the other line.

Peter: In the company you owned, did the admin person have a particular way they answered the phone, or a script they used all the time? How did that happen?

Jason: You want to make sure they have a script where it's going to go through a whole questionnaire process of how did you hear about us? How long have you been thinking about getting the work done? How do you intend to pay for the job? Have you had other estimates? And get as much information as you possibly can so that the salesperson has as much information as they can get to arm themselves to get the deal.

Peter: I guess what you did is you must have developed a questionnaire for your admin person to ask those questions. Is that kind of what you did?

Jason: That's correct. For sure you have a script. You don't want to be off-the-cuff; you don't want to leave anything to chance; you want to make sure you tweak a questionnaire that's catering to your business very specifically.

It does several things: It arms your salesperson when they go to the appointment. If they're going to do it by credit, then you know you've got to be prepared to talk about credit. If they say they're going to do it by cash, that's all good information to know. But if they tell you, "We heard about you through

Valpak," then you know to make an investment in Valpak.

So you can add all that up. You know where all your marketing dollars are going, and what's successful and what's not, so that's going to help the company overall.

Peter: I used to do that too. We used to do Money Mailer, Valpak, the coupon mags and all that kind of stuff. Were you classifying or categorizing based on where they came through as to the type of customer they were?

If you're doing Google PPC with a five bid process, versus maybe a high-end home magazine, I found your clientele is a little bit different. So did you do some categorization like that so you kind of knew what you were dealing with, and how price sensitive it would be?

Jason: For sure. Naturally everybody wants to do that.

One thing I know – and anybody who's been in the business for any period of time – you almost can't prequalify, as much as you want to. Oh man, that came from a high dollar magazine. But then they get the cheapest windows or cheapest siding on a house.

How call backs kill your business!

You go to a customer, who called you from a newspaper ad, and they're in a part of town you don't want to be in at 6:00 at night but you go. But then they get the highest quality stuff. So you can never prequalify any lead – that's for sure.

Peter: You never know. Throughout this book I'm going to ask Jason these things, or what I call "red flags" or "objections." The first red flag that comes up here in this part of the process is how do you teach your admin person (the extension of you, the salesperson) [how to respond] if they ask if both spouses are going to be there and they say, "No, they can't. My husband's busy – he works too much. But I'm the decision-maker anyway."

Jason: That's probably one of the more difficult things, because nobody wants to be the bad guy. But I have to say that if you don't have both spouses there, you're certainly not getting the business the night you're going to be there.

Because even though they'll almost always say, "I make all the decisions. They don't need to be here," that's really not the point. The point is you want both spouses there, because you don't want to have one spouse try to relay all your information to the other spouse. You want to be able to do it with both.

It goes back to you wouldn't want someone who worked at McDonald's to operate on you; you want a doctor to operate on you. Well, this is the same thing. That spouse doesn't do what you do, so you want to make sure you can have both of them there to give them both the information.

You'd be doing them a disservice if you didn't have them both there, and that's the whole point of that. So if they aren't willing to have both spouses there, I personally wouldn't even run the appointment.

Peter: I felt the same way, because otherwise you've got to backtrack and do two presentations when you can just do one, so I agree with you totally. I think it makes a lot of sense.

Your mindset is I'm going in and I'm going to do what I do. I'm going to do my measuring and present the offer, and try to get the deal closed. But does it have any value if they know which order you're in in order to present certain type of information to create doubt in the customer's mind? Did you ever work that kind of a situation?

Jason: I'm sorry. You have to say the question again.

How call backs kill your business!

Peter: For example, your admin calls and asks, "Are you getting other bids?" "Yeah." "How many?" "I'm getting three."
Then you would ask, "Are we the first or the last bid we're getting? Where do we sit?" Does it matter at all to you which order you come in?

Jason: I'd suggest that if they're getting multiple bids, don't ask that question because it can be offensive. I'd just say if they're going to get multiple bids and they tell you that up front, set your date a little further out than typical so you can make sure you do come in on the tail end of all that.

Peter: Why is that? For all the salespeople who are reading this book, what is the value of being at the tail end and why is it important?

Jason: It's always important. Because when you go in as a salesperson, if you're good enough you'll be able to fact-find, or gather or see samples laying around or whatever, and you'll know who came in there before you. And that further arms you to have an advantage and a distinctive edge over your competition.

Peter: We've both done tons and tons of business. Do you have a story related to being the last one? For example, a previous contractor was in there, and they had convinced the customer to go with them. You were able to bring something up that created doubt in that client's mind for them to want to switch and go with you. Do you have a story like that that you could tell?

Jason: That's a darn good question. Specific stories? It happened all the time. I would always go into homes where they pretty much had their minds made up. It would be really easy to fall into that. Why am I even here if their minds are made up? Well, their mind's not made up if you are there. You have to twist that mindset because they want to hear one more.

You can bring a nice refreshing approach. "If you follow my process..." and you become best friends by the end of the meeting, they're going to reconsider.

You're not always going to get them. There are good salespeople out there. It can be tough to overcome at times. But if you follow my process, you're going to close more of those.

Peter: We'll get into that in the process going forward. I want to tell you guys a quick funny story. Jason's going to speak about this here in this process, and why this is important.

How call backs kill your business!

A lot of times the sale is not about the product or service you're offering: It's about your ability to connect with, build trust, and relate to that person.

This is one of the stories that stands out in the thousands of deals I did. I went into this retired lady's home for a kitchen remodel, and it was a modest home. We'll get into some of the details you talk about here and why it's important.

I knocked on the door and I stepped back. She opened the door, and I came into the front entryway. And there on the left-hand side was this dog. The lady said, "This is my dog, Sammy. I love my dog, Sammy. Would you please pet my dog?"

I went over to pet the dog, and I realized the dog wasn't alive – it was stuffed.

Jason: Wow!

Peter: I said, "Okay." I was petting her dog, Sammy, and I thought, *Maybe this lady is a little wacko*. But I kept going.

Then we sat at the kitchen table, and just like you're going to talk about here in the future when we go through this she had all kinds of pictures of her pets and the family. We started talking about that for 20 minutes or so. I did a quick estimate and presented it to her, and walked away with the order.

When I was leaving she said, "You know, you are the only one who bothered to find out about me and about the things I care about. I love my family. I'm remodeling this kitchen [because Thanksgiving was coming up] because we're going to have a big family get-together, and I can see what it's going to look like to have all my family here." That's what closed the deal.

I'm sure you have story after story like that. But that's exactly what happened.

Jason: I have many of those. You just have to dial in on their hot buttons. If you stay on their hot buttons long enough – and it can be completely off-topic – because many salespeople go into a house and just stay on-topic. They never get off-topic. They never relate to the customer, so they don't get their business. They think, *What did I do wrong?* Well, they're not paying attention.

Peter: We'll dive into that a little bit more. So red flag number one: Like Jason said, teach your people who are collecting the information to get as much as they can. And make sure both spouses are there.

We'll talk more about this whole value proposition, because it's not just about what you're selling; it's about what you're saying and how you're connecting as well.

Jason, let's go to the next step in the process. Now you have the lead and you're heading to the appointment. So what happens next?

Jason: You're to make sure you're on time — that's crucial. I do have stories about that. You want to make sure you're on time, but you don't want to be too early. Let's say you have a 4:00 appointment. If you show up 15-20 minutes early, they can be annoyed by that. They were going about their day until [they realized], "We've got a half-hour before the appointment. Let's clean up because we don't want our house to look unsightly when they walk into the house."

So then they start cleaning up. They're doing dishes; they're putting clothes away; they're getting the dogs managed and taking the dogs out so there are no distractions when you get there. If you get there too early, now they're kind of annoyed because they didn't get everything done before you showed up. And they're looking at their watch going, *Man, we said 4:00. Why is he here so early?*

Generally, when you go into meetings that's acceptable. You want to be 10-15 minutes early. If you're not 10 minutes early, you're late. But in this case you don't want to be too early; you want to be five minutes early. I found five minutes early is really that sweet spot. Knock on that door five minutes till.

You don't take any chances. You show up right at 4:00, and they look at their watch and they're like, *He's 30 seconds late. He's not going to be on time. He's right on time – that's not on time in my book.* You'll have those people. But if you're five minutes early there's nothing that can be disputed.

Peter: That's good. One of the things I did for myself (and I taught my general managers and all my employees this), I don't care whether you're on time or you're going to be late. In different parts of the country there's traffic, car accidents happen and things like that. So you always call ten minutes before and let them know if you're going to be on time, or if you're running late and why. And your estimated time of arrival.

People used to tell me all the time they loved that, just to have that communication process. I like your five minutes and not any more because you will create a stressful situation for them. And now you're going to have to deal with their stress or their annoyance on top of it.

Jason: For sure. There are unforeseen things like traffic conditions. Some people live in busier areas than others. You try to hit a 6:00 appointment, and you're hitting rush hour traffic. If you are late you didn't leave enough time, or there was an accident. It could be anything.

Most people who live in those areas understand. But they certainly want a phone call; they don't want you to just show up late, because then that's even more of an annoyance.

Peter: Exactly. What's a good story you have about being too early or too late?

Jason: When I was first doing this business I lived in Virginia Beach. I had a call for an appointment on the peninsula. I left way early. If anybody lives in that area, they could tell you that the Hampton Roads Bridge-Tunnel can be a nightmare at times. It was for me on this particular day. I had a 4:00 appointment. I was on my way and I had plenty of time. I thought I had so much time I could get a bite to eat before the appointment. I didn't know how I was going to kill time when I got to the other side of the bridge.

Well, there was a breakdown, and when there's a breakdown in a bridge-tunnel you're stuck. There's no way around it.

I got to the appointment one minute late. The guy was already standing out on his lawn staring at his watch. His arms were crossed, and he pointed to his watch when I was getting out of my car. And the first words out of his mouth were, "You're late!" I could already tell this was starting off on a bad foot.

But like any salesperson, if you've got a valuable lead you want to make sure you salvage it the best you can. He kept harping and harping on it. And he goes, "You might as well leave. You're late. I don't want to deal with you." There was no way to salvage it.

Sometimes you're going to run into things like that. That was something I couldn't control, but usually you can control it. You definitely don't want to be late.

Peter: Did you call to let him know you were stuck in the tunnel? Maybe that was before cellphones – I don't know.

Jason: I did call but he never answered his phone, so there was nothing I could do about it. I tried several times, but what can you do? Some people just don't understand, and it just boils down to their personality.

Peter: I've had that happen too. Sometimes you can't control traffic, and if they don't

Jason: I had one more story. I arrived super early and had nowhere to go. I wound up saying, *Oh, let me just go and get in here, so* I went up to the door. The lady came out, and she wasn't expecting me to be so early. She was in a robe, I was super uncomfortable, and her husband was still on his way. So don't be early.

Peter: There you go. That's a great story for not being early. I like your five-minute window and call ahead of time. Those are really good things to do. And again, it demonstrates your professionalism and the company you represent.

People really like it. I had more than a couple people tell me part of the reason why we got the work was that our communication was impeccable, and that we always called to let them know where we were at and when we were coming.

The thing we have to remember – especially you guys who are in sales – is people's time is valuable. Just because you're coming doesn't mean they don't have other things going on in their life (meeting, appointment, phone conference call), especially if it's during the middle of the day. You have to make sure you value that time. So Jason, you're right on with your appointment timing.

Now let's move over to the "look and feel of you." You talk a lot about cleanliness and hygiene, so maybe talk a little bit about how should a salesperson look?

I'll tell you a quick story before we get into this. We just moved and we're putting down new carpeting in the home. I had called one of the big box stores to come in. The guy shows up about five minutes late – he did not call. He came in a wrinkled company uniform shirt; he had long, hippy-like hair; and a five-day growth beard on his face.

We didn't go with him. I didn't even want this guy to come into my home, let alone to work with this company and have them do the job. As a previous contractor I was thinking, *Why would you let someone looking like that represent your company?* It's just amazing to me. So maybe you could speak to that a little bit here.

Jason: You were talking earlier that sometimes contractor sales get a bad rep. There's a lot of that out there. A lot of these folks are doubling up as owner/installer. They show up to the job and they're thinking they're just going to give a price.

But usually customers want a little time with you. They're making a big purchase, and they need questions answered. If you don't show up like you want their business, then they make their decision before you even get started.

Peter: What are your rules of thumb? Some small-time operators (and also you guys who are reading this book) are doing a dual role as general contractor/owner, but you're also the salesperson. I don't think you should be showing up with a bunch of dirty work clothes on at the end of the day to do a bid. I don't think that would leave a good impression.

Jason: Correct. You want to make sure you're clean. If you have to, keep an extra shirt handy. Do your job. Go clean up. Put on that nice shirt, and try to look as presentable as you can if you're playing that dual role. It's sometimes difficult to do, but you definitely don't want to walk in there all wrinkled up. And if, heaven forbid, they ask you to take your shoes off at the door.

You want to make sure that if you're going to a sales appointment you know how valuable that is. So you want to take every opportunity to clean yourself up and go in as presentable as possible.

You don't want holes in your socks; you want to be able to offer to take your shoes off. You're going to ask that question when you walk through the door: "Would you like me to take my shoes off?" I've even seen people who would bring booties and say, "I could put booties on when I walk through your house."

It's nice to look like a contractor or an installer because you're perceived as the expert in the field when you are. But you also want to come in with a little bit of authority and as a little bit of an expert so you can thoroughly field their questions, and that they feel confident in you. A lot of that goes back to that impression which means everything.

Peter: Just like we always talk about guys; sales is not about one presentation; sales is about a series of small commitments along the way. So Jason talking about the admin getting the commitment for the appointment, making sure you show up on time, and demonstrating your professionalism shows commitment to the company. Coming in looking clean and offering to put on booties is another commitment. These are all things people notice.

You've got to ask yourself if you were having someone over to your house who was a general contractor (even though you're in sales and you're doing home service sales or you're a general contractor), would you expect the same? And the answer is yes, you would.

I have a quick story on that. I had a painter come in the other day, Jason. It was a small operation, a two-man company. They knocked on the door, and when I opened the door we exchanged pleasantries. He immediately pulled out two booties from his briefcase and started putting them on his feet just as a general practice.

His name was Jonathan. I said, "You don't have to do that. Our carpets are old – we're getting them replaced." But the fact that he did that registered in my mind that this guy is very professional and positive for that commitment. So it does matter what you're saying.

Jason: Those small things do add up. They really do register with the homeowner, especially the lady of the house who's the one who will take notice of all the details. Men generally don't pick up on the same things that some of the ladies do. But they do appreciate it because the home is very meaningful to the ladies.

When you do things like that, it looks like you've been around the block. It looks like you know what you're doing and you're a professional.

Peter: Who's typically the key decision-maker out of the man and the woman?

Jason: Oh, it's always the woman. She's the one who makes all the decisions. The man tries to persuade and pitch arguments for or against, but ultimately the decision almost always up to the lady.

Peter: We were talking about cologne, perfume or sense of smells.

Jason: Going back to those contractors, they'll try to clean up and they'll put a little cologne on so they can mask being in the field all day. But I'll tell you, if you walk into a house and they smell that cologne, that's all they can think about and they associate that smell.

You want to eliminate all the things that distract from or take away focus from the sale. In some cases, if they don't like the cologne or the perfume -- and they find it offensive and they're gagging the whole time because you put too much on – you just don't want to take those chances. In some cases, they could have allergic reactions to it. So you definitely want to eliminate all possibilities of having those obstacles get in your way of getting the deal.

Peter: Going back to the story I mentioned about the guy with the long hair, what's your take as far as haircuts and beards?

(The other thing we've got to talk about are tattoos, because that's a pretty common thing among the younger generation, but not so common among some of the Baby Boomers). Maybe you could speak to that a little bit, Jason.

Jason: Some of the older customers you might have would take serious offense to those things. You might not think it's a big deal, but to have a ZZ Top beard – all those things make you look suspicious, and you start taking away from looking like an expert. I know it sounds small and petty, but all these things added up will help you in the long-run.

So make sure you keep your beard, if you have one, clean-cut, even and don't have stragglers. If you have long hair, tie it back real nice. You don't want all these distractions because they are all distractions, especially to an older couple. Younger folks it's not as big of a deal.

I've had salespeople who had tattoos down their arms, so they would have to wear long sleeves. I didn't want to chance the appointments because they had tattoos on their arms. So I would suggest if you have tattoos to wear long sleeves – even if it's hot outside – and cover that stuff up, because it is a distraction.

Peter: I totally agree. I used to tell guys in my company all the time, "This is nothing against you, and I have nothing against tattoos. But if you come into a home and it's an older lady, if those tattoos would scare your mom they're going to scare that older lady, so you've got to cover them up." That was the policy we had in our company.

It's not whether I think tattoos are good or bad. I'd always tell my general managers or the sales guys, "If you don't do these kinds of things, you're actually taking money out of your own pocket because you're not closing as many sales and you're not getting the commission. So wouldn't it make sense for you to want to do this to make more money in your bank account?"

Jason: If think if you put that way it makes sense.

Peter: Now, let's move on. We previously talked about the stuffed dog in the book, and I'm sure we both have crazy stories we could tell. We could do a whole book just on crazy stories.

Jason: Oh, man. I tell you – you're right about that. I've seen some crazy ones.

Peter: Maybe we should do that. That actually would be a pretty funny book. Maybe we'll offer that as a bonus, *The Top 50*

Crazy Stories, because I'm sure we've seen it all.

I want to ask you about what to look for when you're in the home, and this gets back to what Jason and I were talking about. Many times if you're selling siding, windows, doors, roofing, kitchen and bath remodels, selling is not based on what you do; it's based on how you're connecting with that person and letting them talk.

So what do you look for? How do you engage people, and why is that important?

Jason: When you get out of the car, immediately you start surveying where you are, the neighborhood and the school systems – you want to think about all that stuff.

You want to look for any yard signs or anything they're into. If they have a Marine flag out front, or "13.1" and "26.2" on their window. Or if they have some crazy bumper sticker or a school system bumper sticker (is an honor roll student) or something like that. All those things help you, because when you get in their arms are crossed and the walls are up.

So you've got to break the walls down and uncross their arms by relating to them and asking personal questions, assuming they have the personality to receive that. Some folks just want to get right to business. But you have to be able to dial in on that personality.

A lot of those things are going to help you walk through the living room. You're going to see golf trophies, framed certificates or family photos. They have all kinds of things on display because they like to talk about them. So when you get to the kitchen table that first 15-20 minutes, that warm-up time, is going to be all about breaking those walls down to get their trust.

Peter: I want to go through a sample dialogue of how that sounds like with you in just a second. But before we do that I want to back up just a second. You took the appointment, you got yourself all ready to go, and you arrived five minutes earlier on time.

But there are a couple other really important steps I want to make sure we don't miss. Jason, can you talk about when you're going up the sidewalk to the door, how do you approach the door? Where do you stand? These are all important things I think you need to share with the people who are reading this.

Jason: A lot of folks will have a side light to the door. So you're going to go up to the door but you're not going to ring the doorbell. I always say "friends knock – strangers ring the doorbell." So don't ring the doorbell, because then you're already perceived as a stranger. It reinforces, *Oh, there's a stranger at my door.*

You want to knock on the door. It really is all about the psychology behind it. You knock on the door, you step down off the first step, and you make sure you're in view of the side light so they can see you as they're approaching the door. When they open the door you're down a little bit, so they're looking down on you and you have a smile on your face.

It's all psychology because you're trying to get them into a very positive mindset when they meet you. So then you immediately shake their hand – firmly, not limply. You look them straight in the eye and you smile, and you thank them for having you over.

Peter: That's good. One of the things I told my guys is never stand right on top of the door, because when they open the door you're taking that psychologically aggressive role, and it can be scary sometimes. So I like your idea of stepping back off the porch just so you're not in their face.

The other thing I want to ask you, you had the admin calling and they set the appointment. Did you ever call the day before to confirm your appointment? How did that all happen?

Jason: I would always call the day before. I didn't want to leave anything to chance where I show up and one spouse is there. Or they forgot they had the appointment, and then you're showing up and they're kind of out of sorts.

So you make sure you call the day before. It's a courtesy call. Like you said before, you want to put yourself in their shoes. You would like a courtesy call.

What's even better about that is you get a chance to give that first impression. "Hey, my name is Jason Blevins. I just want to let you know that I'll be the guy coming out to see you tomorrow at 4:00. Here's my number, and I'll see you then. Do you have any questions for me before I show up? Is this appointment still good?"

You want to get that cleared up [ahead of time]. If they say, "We already signed a contract with somebody three days ago. I meant to call you back. Boy, it's a good thing you called," because then you can set an appointment to go somewhere else and actually make some money.

Peter: The other thing I find so important about that is when Jason calls and says, "Hi, my name is Jason Blevins. I'm the guy who's going to be at your appointment." Then when you show up and they open the door and you say, "Hi, I'm Jason Blevins," they remember your voice and now they're seeing your face and they go, "Oh, nice to meet you." So you're starting to build rapport and trust.

So I think it's so important to make that call the day or night before. Not only to know the appointment is still good; but to start establishing that connect they have with you.

Jason: Right. And even if it's, say, an older couple or a single lady, it's always a courtesy to let them know that you're the one who's showing up so they can expect you, and they can put a name to the person who's coming to their door.

Peter: Yes, that's very important. So let's fast-forward to where we were. Let's say you walk into a home. Now you're in the home, and the husband and wife are there. Let's say it's an older, retired couple, and they're in a golf resort community. You notice a bunch of golf stuff and you think, *Okay, somebody in here likes to golf.*

What would be a question or two to start the conversation the golf warm-up? What would you do there?

Jason: I might ask them if they played a certain course, or if they're a scratch golfer, or what's their handicap and how often they get to play. "Oh, by the way, if we can do business together maybe I'll take you golfing one day," to let them know that there might be golfing in this for you if you do business with me. Just little things like that.

Peter: For the guys who are reading this, here are a couple key things from listening to things Jason did really well as a salesperson:

1. You're connecting with a person and their passion. They might say, "Oh yeah, we golf as a couple. We travel all over the country, and we go to all these different big courses and we love to do that. We have an RV." So they'll start talking with you, and you can go down that course with them to warm them up, like Jason's talking about.

2. When you ask are you a scratch golfer or what's your handicap, people love to brag about themselves. And if they're good, they'll tell you. Right, Jason?

How call backs kill your business!

Jason: That's right. And if they're bad, they'll tell you that too.

Peter: Then the third thing Jason did is it's a way to create an outstanding customer service experience: "When I get these guys signed up on the contract, I'm going to take them out for a morning or afternoon game of golf." And that would be done as something you'd do as a way to say thank you for the business.

I'll tell you what, Jason – and I'm sure you've done this before – by doing that you blow those people away so much that they're going to tell everybody about the golfing time they had with you, and what a cool guy this guy is. "If you ever need to get your siding done, I'd definitely recommend you go to these guys. And who knows, maybe he'll take you golfing too."

Jason: Then on top of that you say, "Hey, let's do a foursome. Invite a couple of your buddies to go with us." And now you've got a couple potential referrals.

Peter: There you go. We're going to get into some of your tricks on the trade on the backside here of how you bring in the neighbors. But one thing as it relates to what Jason was talking about (this is so important, guys. Jason's got some really cool tactics down in the back there we'll talk about), typically where people live like attracts like. And neighborhoods typically have similar type of people who live there with similar type of interests.

For this example, if it's a golf resort community, well, guess what? Probably a lot of people who are there like golf. So if Jason's taking a foursome out for golf, there are other people who can come along because they have that same interest.

The other thing I want to point out, Jason – and I'm sure you do this too because you make a mental note, and we'll talk about the pamphlet stuff you do at the back side because that's very important – the key thing to remember is houses in a neighborhood were typically built the same time as a tract situation. So if one neighbor has a siding issue, probably a few neighbors around the area have similar siding issues because that builder used the same material at the same particular time on the application. Wouldn't you agree, Jason?

Jason: Oh, yeah. You're actually kind of reading my mind right now. If someone's getting their siding replaced it's usually because it's time, which means that for everybody in the neighborhood, it's probably time as well.

I think it's a great practice that if you get someone's business and you get the contract signed to let that customer know that hey, I'm going to walk around and let your neighbors know I'm going to be doing business for you. And to contact me if there are any issues or noise so you don't have to deal with it. I can field that for you.

They appreciate that. And now they know you're going to walk around the neighborhood so they don't wonder why is he doing this? Why is he walking the neighborhood? Now they know what you're doing.

You go up to all the neighbors and let them know, "Hey, my name's Jason Blevins. I'm with so-and-so company. Here's my card. I'm doing business for your neighbor down the street here. And I just wanted to let you know that if there are any issues, if they're being too noisy, if there's trash that rolls into your yard, or if there's anything you're not happy with, just please give me a call and I'll come out and take care of it myself personally.

"I own the business, and just so you know if you ever need any services down the road just give me a call and I'll be happy to come out and give you a free estimate."

Peter: That's perfect, that's awesome. I would imagine you probably got some good business out of that over the time when you had your own business.

Jason: Oh, yeah. If it never worked, I wouldn't do it. But it did work and I did get business. That's something a lot of sales reps neglect. They go to their lead, they get the business and they leave. And they neglect all the juicy opportunities around it.

Peter: I guess you call that "pamphlet marketing," and we'll have a section on that as well. But that's what you're referring to: You just go over and talk to them and hand out your pamphlet and away you go.

Jason: A lot of companies will have a brochure with their product offerings. Or at the very least the sales rep can bring them a business card, or maybe a brochure or some literature for the siding they're putting on the neighbor's house. So they say, "Hey, here's this nice insulated panel siding. Look at this stuff. Here's my business card. This is what's going up. If you have any questions, call me."

It's always nice to connect and reach out. Once you get one or two of those guys that neighborhood starts becoming your neighborhood.

Peter: That's very cool. Again, a lot of business and entrepreneurial gurus talk about the lifetime value of the customer. I used to always talk about it as the "lifetime value of the neighborhood," because there's a lot of business to be had in a neighborhood.

So you're in the home, and you're warming up and talking about their interests. You mentioned a term you use called "chameleonizing." Could you talk a little bit about what the heck that is?

Jason: I thought I coined "chameleonizing," but I've heard other sales presentations and people speak the same word, so maybe I didn't. But basically it's just making yourself like your customer. People deal with people who are like themselves. And they find that people who are like themselves are more relatable because they understand them better.

So if you come to a customer who is straight to business – let's say an engineer who wants the facts – you become Mr. Fact Man and get straight to the point. There's not a lot of warm-up time there.

But once you start breaking the walls down and you get to the kitchen table, let's say you have a pitch book and you turn to something that interests them. If they sit up in their chair and they're really interested in it, you sit up in your chair and you mirror them. You just discovered a hot button, so you can really harp on that and really reel them in with that. If they lay back and they're looking comfortable, you lay back and look comfortable. You just have to mirror them.

So think "chameleonize." If I have someone who has a Southern accent and they're not from these parts, the next thing you know I'd develop a serious twang in my speech. It's just the way it works out. I wind up chameleonizing myself unconsciously. I don't even think about it, it's just natural for me.

Peter: That is very cool. I've done a lot of interesting work in personality types, Jason is right on. We'll give a reference in the book here about the Disc profile. And then there are four personality types:

1. Driver, which is the let's get down to business and what's the bottom line – Jason is talking about that.

2. The influencer or the high I. Typically a lot of salespeople are high I's. These people want to be the center of attention and they want to have fun, so you chameleonize that.

3. Amiable who are all about connection and relationships, so you're really going to talk to them a long time about their family and their interests.

4. Then the one Jason mentioned – the engineer or the scientists – are the analytics, and they need to see everything under the sun. They want to see all your processes, procedures and everything you can lay out for them, so you've got to pummel them to death with facts and figures and processes because that's what they love to see and that builds value.

So know the personality type, and we'll provide some more resources for you so you can recognize these people. For instance, we talk about the nerdy engineer with the pocket protector (that's kind of an extreme situation).

But people kind of tip their hand by some of the things they say. Like Jason said, "Hey, can we just get to the bottom line here? So what's the deal?" That's a driver – it's all about the bottom line.

Jason, have you done work in the area of eye movements and watching what the eyes are doing when you're talking to people as far as chameleonizing?

Jason: That all boils down to body language and positioning. I talk a little bit about positioning the couple or the spouses in front of you.

If you put them on the left and right side of you, you're losing the battle because they're able to communicate without even talking. A lot of that is their eyes while looking at each other. If they're rolling or they're down. Or they're open real wide they're excited about it, like this seems like a good deal. All that stuff is being missed.

I talk a little bit about if anybody plays poker they know for sure when someone is getting ready to make a bid, or they're getting ready to fold. Whenever it's on that person, everybody is staring at their face because they're looking at every little tell, every little opportunity to see if they have a hand or are they bluffing? Anyone who plays poker a weaker opponent is going to give it away, so everybody will know how to play against that hand.

The same thing here: You're basically playing poker. You're at the kitchen table, and you want to make sure you get them both in front of you because now you're playing two opponents and not just one.

So you've got to get all of that. You can't let any of that slip, so pay attention. If their eyes widen when you're talking about something, that's a tell-tale sign they're excited about it. So get on top of that and hit on that hot button.

Peter: Jason will provide a bonus section for you, but I'm just going to quickly touch on it. He'll get into more detail on this, but one of the things I always watched for is eye movement and these are just some of the basics.

Basically it's involuntary, which means the eyes move without them controlling them. This is why Jason said to have them be in view of you so you can see what's going on while they're talking to you. If their eye movement is side-to-side from ear-to-ear, they're recalling a conversation that could have been with a previous contractor a significant other while sitting at the table. You know that's something where they had a conversation, so you can delve into that.

If their eyes go up involuntarily, they're recalling a thought or memory so you can delve into that a little bit more.

If you're asking something and their eyes go down towards their heart, they're having some kind of an emotional connection. So that's where you want to bring that out a little bit more and talk about "How does that make you feel?" because there's something going on there with the emotion of it.

Again, we read body language and eye movement to build that trust and connection that Jason is talking about. So he'll have some more about that later on in the book and in this video course.

Jason: Two quick thoughts if you don't mind. You're talking about emotion. If you can get them to where they're almost in a childlike emotion about what you're talking about – and they get a little giddy, a little childish, and they go back to that feeling of they're actually going to get something they want that they're really excited about – that is a good, sweet spot in a sales process if you can master how to get them to that childlike feeling.

On a side note, a bad eye movement would be to their watch.

Peter: Exactly, if they're always looking down. That's very true. As long as you brought that up, let's talk about that.

If they start looking at their watch, how do you deal with that? What do you do?

Jason: Well, if they're looking at their watch that's a bad thing because you're doing something wrong. You're not keying in on the hot topics; you're keying in on things that don't matter to them. Now, it might matter to you and you might think it's important. But you need to get off whatever you're talking about and move on to something else.

Peter: One other thing I talk about in some of my sales courses is if you want to get them refocused, one of the best ways to do that is to say, "Hey, can I ask you a question?" and then wait until they look back up at you. Then you can move into another line of questioning, like Jason is talking about, to refocus them and get them back on track. So that's very important.

I'm glad you brought the childlike state up. One of the things I was taught a long time ago by this guy who was a real salty old salesperson. "You know, if you're ever worried about dealing with people who have a really gruff exterior, every time you go on a sales call always remember that everyone who's an adult was a kid one time. Looking at them like when they were a kid changes your whole mentality." And he's right – that's a pretty cool way to look at it.

Jason: Exactly.

Peter: Let's keep moving. We're going to get into time management in just a second. But you brought up a really important point a few minutes ago about where you should be in the house (i.e., a kitchen table versus the living room or other places). Can you talk about why that's so important to be in any particular room in the house?

Jason: I've always said that the kitchen table is where business is done. The living room is where people go to relax. They kick back and watch TV. Their unconscious mindset in that room is not business. But their mindset in the kitchen is business at the table, and that's where you can spread all your stuff out – samples, brochures, science experiment if you have one, like a window testing kit or something like that.

That's where all the business is done. That's where the least amount of distraction is, that's where people cook their meals and they get out, and that's where they socialize. If you ever notice at parties, they end up migrating to the kitchen.

That's where business is done. If you go into the living room, it's too easy to get comfortable. It's too easy to look out the windows and see all the distractions.

They might have the TV running, so you want to turn the TV off. You want to have music not playing in the background. You want to eliminate all the possible distractions so that they can maintain focus on what you have to say.

Peter: Let's say they're motioning to go into the living room and sit down on the couch. How do you get them to move over to the kitchen? What do you do?

Jason: It really doesn't have to be so complicated. Just say, "I don't want to inconvenience you. But would you be okay if we take this to the kitchen table?" They'll say, "Oh, sure. Yeah." But if they start giving you pushback, then don't force the issue.

Usually they'll want to go to the kitchen table, especially if they've had other estimates, because the other salespeople have taken them there and that's where they're used to going.

You don't want to do it in the living room if you can help it. If you have to, that's fine – do your business. But this is all about increasing your chances and stacking all the opportunities in your favor, so move it to the kitchen table if you can.

Peter: Sounds good. I think that's a smart move, and that's what I always used to do too. Before you do the warm-up, so to speak, in the bull pen here, what about time management? How do you handle that with people so you don't overstay your welcome? What do you do there?

Jason: A lot of this stuff you don't want to guess – you just ask. "I know we have a 4:00 appointment, but we didn't set any time-frames. Can you tell me how much time I have to share with you today?" They'll tell you, "As long as you need," which is great.

If they tell you "as long as you need," they don't mean four hours. If they tell you "as long as you need" say, "If I can be in and out in an hour-and-a-half, is that okay with you?" You want to be respectful of their time and let them know everything up front so that they're not surprised later or looking at their watch later.

No matter how much they like your content, they don't want to see you for four hours.

Peter: Got it. But I've got to ask this question because this does happen, so I want to cover it since you're the expert. What if they say, "You've got 45 minutes because we got another contractor lined up right behind you." What do you do then?

Jason: Forty-five minutes isn't enough time to close a deal. And if they have a contractor coming behind you say, "Great. I had something come up. I was kind of worried because I wasn't sure how I was going to cover two things at once. This works out perfect for me. Would you be okay if we set this for another time where I can have a little more time – maybe an hour-and-a-half – instead of 45 minutes? Are you okay with that?"

Let that other guy come in, then that way you can come in behind the other sales rep. Because in my opinion 45 minutes is not enough time to close a deal.

Peter: What do you typically need? At least an hour to an hour-and-a-half, 60 to 90 minutes?

Jason: I would say an hour-and-a-half is a nice sweet spot. You can get a contract done and signed within an hour-and-a-half to two hours. In an hour-and-a-half you're going to get through your process if you get their business. And then you want to cool down with them, so I would say two hours is a nice block of time. Beyond that you want to get out the door.

Peter: I guess backing up and going further upstream, is that something you have the admin ask? "We're looking for about two hours of your time. Would that be okay?" Do you ask that when you're setting up the appointment?

Jason: That would actually be a very good thing to put on that questionnaire. You want to contour that questionnaire to your company, but almost always you want to see if you can get a good solid block of time. You don't want them to dictate it on the other end.

Peter: If you do a lot of bids and things like Jason has done, you're going to get into some potential prospective clients who are a little crafty. They'll say one thing to the admin, and then you come in and get the bomb dropped on you. "I've got another contractor coming in 45 minutes after you," when they said the appointment would be two hours.

So Jason, I like the fact that you politely excuse yourself and come in on the back side. That's the best way to do it, instead of trying to rush through your presentation because that never works.

Jason: Well, if you rush through it one, you're eliminating a paycheck to yourself, and your increasing the chances for the salesperson behind you. And two, you're doing a disservice to that homeowner. If you truly care about the person you're dealing with, you want to make sure you don't do them a disservice; you want to give them the same service and quality you give everybody else.

Peter: That's very true. You can't demonstrate your professionalism when you're rushed, so I totally agree.

How call backs kill your business!

One Day Workshops & Online Courses

As the owner of a remodeling business, have you ever wondered...
- Why is it so hard to find good salespeople?
- How do I retain good salespeople?
- How do I get out of working in my business to working on my business?
- How can I increase my sales numbers through my team?
- How can I get my team's closing ratio up?
- Is there a process that can be duplicated?
- How can I get my sales team to get the deal on the first visit?
- How can I get an edge over my competition?
- How can my team pick up some leads on their own?

What if you could...
- Hire and keep good salespeople
- Free time up for yourself and put energy into your business
- Put more money towards your bottom line
- Get a greater return on investment with your marketing dollars
- Strike fear in the hearts of your competition!

Remember when selling in the home used to be fun? What happened? Why are business owners working so hard just to keep the lights on? The One Day Close was created, field tested and mastered to bring back a selling process that has been lost over the years of a down economy. It's time to make money at this thing again. In fact, it's time your company has a break-out year. With The One Day Close system, you can do just that.

www.theonedayclose.com   (717)292-8686

Chapter 2: The Process

"The Process" is where the chess match begins. These critical steps will be your foundation to executing a beautiful sale. Although it takes some time to master, once you get good at this step, you will truly enjoy your craft. "The Process" takes the end user on a journey into your world. This should be a fun and exciting experience but all too often, this is where the salesperson lacks confidence and is full of frustration because the end user is beating them up. This chapter will guide you through the exact methods and timing throughout the entire sales process. We dive deeper into the reasons behind the necessity of precise execution.

Peter: Now let's go over the warm-up. You're at the kitchen table, and you're starting the whole dialogue process. You've talked about their pets, family, golf or whatever, so what's next? How does this whole warm-up start?

Jason: Going back to the chameleonizing, the warm-up is if they're looking relaxed, you look relaxed. And you want to treat them like a friend, like you've known them for a little while. And you want them to perceive you as a friend, so you're going to play catch-up.

"How have things been? When I walked up I saw that you have a Purdue University sticker out there. I'm from Lafayette. Did you guys go to Purdue? Who went to Purdue?"

"My kid's going to Purdue right now for agriculture."

"Oh, that's fantastic. What year are they in?"

"They're a junior."

"How are they doing? Are they liking it? Do they like the area? Are they going to move back?

You want to engage in conversation and get off-topic to let them relax and perceive you as a friend.

Peter: Then what's next? Do you explain to them how the process is going to go? What happens there?

Jason: If you read their body language and get a feel for their personality, you'll realize when it's time to dive into your process.

The next piece of that would be kind of a questionnaire: "Really quick, I'm just going to ask you a few questions just so I can get on the same page with you and make sure I'm giving you what you're looking for today."

So you just ask them a few questions. You break out a piece of a paper and start drilling down a questionnaire and asking them all the things that are applicable to the appointment. The same kind of things you'd ask when the admin person took the call to begin with.

The whole point of that is to show them you care, that you're trying to get in tune with them, and that you want to bring value to what they're looking for. You don't want to give them a bunch of filler; you want to dial in on what their needs are, and that's important to the customer.

Peter: The other thing I've found over the years is between the time when your admin talked to them and when you talked to them, they may have talked amongst each other and said, "We told your admin that we were looking to get siding. But we also realized our windows are getting pretty old, so we want to look at getting windows to go along with the siding." You'll never know unless you go through that and ask.

Jason: Right. So things do change. If you set the appointment out in that one-week timeframe, other salespeople might have been in there. They might have spurred other thoughts, and now you might have some new information to feed on.

Peter: That's really key. So you're reviewing the questionnaire, and then what's next? Do you talk about what you plan to do while you're there? What's your next step?

Jason: The next step is to give them a breakdown of what I plan to do and what my process is so they're familiar with everything I'm going to do. Plus, it also kind of gives them a timetable. So I tell them, "I'm going to do this questionnaire. And I'm going to tell you a little bit about my business so you have confidence in my company," because that's important, right?

You're going to be doing the whole "yes nod" thing throughout the whole thing. You're closing throughout the whole sales process.

So you're going to tell them about the company. "I'm going to tell you a little bit about some of the product offerings we have, and then I'm going to go measure. Then when I come back in I'm going to give you a price. So when I give you that price and when that is all done, then I'm going to ask for your business." And then you pause.

They may smile, or they may say, "We have other estimates." All those objections at that point is not the time to answer them. You're going to be covering any possible objections they might have through your sales process.

Once they start giving you objections, if you do it upfront at the beginning and start covering those objections first, then it starts taking you off offense and puts you more on defense. It's a lot harder to score on defense, so you want to maintain a position of being on the offense with your customer and guide the whole process.

Even if they give you an objection, you don't want to respond to it – you just move on and hopefully that's all covered through your process at the end where there's nothing left to talk about. There are no more objections and you can get their business.

Peter: I can't stress enough how important what you just brought up is: To let them know that you are going to be asking for their business at the end to set that expectation. Many salespeople come in and go through the whole process. But they don't ask for the business at the end, and then they wonder why they can't write a bunch of orders and get better commissions.

Jason: Not only that, sometimes they *do* ask for their business at the end, but the customer wasn't expecting it. This way you get it out of the way upfront, and you let them know that "...at the end I will be asking for your business."

Whether they have objections, or whether they have other estimates coming – it doesn't matter. You told them you were going to ask, and you're going to stay true to your commitments to them, and you're going to stay true to your word. They know you're an honest person, so at the end they expect you to ask for their business.

Peter: A very important piece of this is don't go through all the work. Make sure you tell them ahead of time. And then ask for it at the very end because they're expecting it – like Jason said – and you deserve to ask because you did all the work to go through that process.

Jason, you talked about the questionnaire. Now you're going to get into I guess a little bit of your company story. What do you want to talk about that's important to share with a potential client?

Jason: Not only do they need to have trust and confidence in you; but they need to have trust and confidence in the company they're dealing with.

They want to make sure you have a good track record. They don't want to hear your company, after further review, has multiple complaints at the Better Business Bureau.

You want to put out there, "We have an A+ rating on the Better Business Bureau. We've been in business for 22 years. We're the leader in this industry in the area. We've won this award; we've won that award. We're part of the Chamber of Commerce, and we have credentials.

"And by the way, here are some testimonial letters from some of my customers. If you need to speak with somebody I have some phone numbers of some folks. If you want to call them and ask about how our service was, they'll be happy to take your call."

Have some folks lined up who are willing to take phone calls on your behalf. If you've really chummed it up with a customer, and you've got a really good rapport, those folks aren't going to have a problem answering a couple calls about how great their experience was.

Peter: That is very true, and especially with testimonials. People view the Better Business Bureau as some kind of an objective force out there. Obviously if you have an A or an A+ rating, you want to let them know about that. And then it's good to have other testimonials as well.

How call backs kill your business!

	In the information you gave to me you mentioned "products and kill pieces." What's that all about?
Jason:	I'm sorry. Ask the question again?
Peter:	The "product and kill pieces." What is that all about? I guess it's getting into your competitor's products and bringing them into the home. What's your view on that?
Jason:	You don't want to specifically call out your competitors because that's negative. That's a bad thing. You want to stay positive throughout your whole approach.

But it's okay to bring in and say, "Here's the competition's panel." So now you're blanketing everybody, but you're not specifically calling anybody out.

Let's say you go in with an insulated siding. I used to take a little Louisville Slugger bat and a can of freeze spray, and I'd spray down a kill piece (which would be a hollow-back piece). And then I'd hit with the bat and it'd break in a million pieces. And then the climb [or claim?] is, "Hey, it gets pretty cold here, right? Oh, man. Imagine if you did this. Well, now look at this piece."

Then I would spray my piece, and I would hit it with the bat over and over and over but it would never break. They were sold! They had to have it on their house.

"Let's face it, you're only going to do siding once. You're never going to replace it again, so why not put the best stuff on your house. Do you want this on there? Would you like to see this on your house if you had a choice?" Obviously you're selling them on your product. They don't want the competition – they want you.

Peter: That makes a lot of sense. You're really kind of building that confidence in your product and that's so key. But more importantly, you're building confidence in them that they're making the right decision on the product choice. That's the key thing there.

Jason: Correct.

Peter: You do all that, so what's next? Are you going to do a measure? What's the next step in the process?

Jason: Like you promised you're going to go out and measure. If you have the husband and wife there, always take the husband. Ask them "Would you mind helping me out?" even if it's just windows. You're not going to just count the windows; you're going to measure every single window. You're really only going to check to see if it's under 101 united inches, and make sure it's not an oversized window.

When you go around, that's showing there's more value. *This guy discounted my windows, but this guy actually went around and measured every window.* So you're being more perceived as the expert, and you're also bringing the husband in to go around and help you.

Then on top of that you're eliminating the opportunity for the husband and wife to be able to bring up all the negative things to have those conversations. You want to see all those interactions, so you take them away from each other so they can't have interactions without you.

Peter: Ah, okay.

Jason: That's one key thing. The other key thing is when you're going around and measuring all the windows, for example, and you put your hand [over a window] and you feel a little bit of a draft between the sash and the frame, it's pretty standard.

If older windows are getting replaced you can feel that and say, "Hey, feel this. Feel this." You engage the husband, and you make them feel like you're all part of the same team and you're coming together for the same mutual result.

Then when you bring that up it's not really a big thing. It's probably because they didn't lock the sash – it could be anything. Now all of a sudden, man, you put a tourniquet on a band-aid. What wasn't a big deal is now a huge deal and now there's a hurricane coming through the house, right?

With that now there's air leakage, which means there's potential for water leakage, which means there's all these other potential structural damages. "Man, you've really got to get these windows replaced," blah-blah-blah.

You take that experience back to the wife. But you let the husband do all the talking, and he starts selling it for you to the wife who again, makes all the decisions.

Peter: Jason, what you bring up is really powerful stuff. And I hope you guys who are reading this pay close attention to what he's saying here.

What is going on with the psychology there between the husband and wife? Why is it important that the husband go around with you, and then explain what he learned from you to the wife? What is going on psychologically there?

Jason: You're giving them the feeling that they're the ones who are on offense; that they're the ones who are leading the sale. You're giving power to the husband, and you get to sit back and watch them be a cheerleader for you.

Peter: That's so powerful. Guys, just to build off what Jason just said, you have to remember that no one ever, ever wants to be sold to – they want to buy, so the husband is creating the buying experience for you.

Plus, men are fixers. We liked to have knowledge about things and fix things. Jason, you're probably that same way around your home, right?

Jason: Oh, exactly. I do it all.

Peter: All guys are [fixers]. We know that. And women typically are the decision-makers in the home, like you had said. So let the guy be the knowledge guy and the fixer, and the woman be the decision-maker. It already exists in the home; just recognize that and use it in your process that Jason's talking about here in order to put them in a buying experience instead of the selling experience. That's the only thing I'm pointing out here.

This is really powerful stuff he's talking about. Taking that husband out and

| | educating him as you go is really building the value. But the psychological power behind that is really intense. So good stuff!

Jason: You're letting the already existing in-home dynamic work for you.

Peter: Exactly. And hopefully that's not a bigger dynamic because you may have to stop a fight. I've had that happen too, but that's an extreme case.

How call backs kill your business!

One Day Workshops & Online Courses

As the owner of a remodeling business, have you ever wondered...
- Why is it so hard to find good salespeople?
- How do I retain good salespeople?
- How do I get out of working in my business to working on my business?
- How can I increase my sales numbers through my team?
- How can I get my team's closing ratio up?
- Is there a process that can be duplicated?
- How can I get my sales team to get the deal on the first visit?
- How can I get an edge over my competition?
- How can my team pick up some leads on their own?

What if you could...
- Hire and keep good salespeople
- Free time up for yourself and put energy into your business
- Put more money towards your bottom line
- Get a greater return on investment with your marketing dollars
- Strike fear in the hearts of your competition!

Remember when selling in the home used to be fun? What happened? Why are business owners working so hard just to keep the lights on? The One Day Close was created, field tested and mastered to bring back a selling process that has been lost over the years of a down economy. It's time to make money at this thing again. In fact, it's time your company has a break-out year. With The One Day Close system, you can do just that.

www.theonedayclose.com   (717)292-8686

Chapter 3: The Close

"The Close" Now is the time. You've run the race and are pushing your chest out to break the finish line tape. Understanding how to close is crucial. A lot of salespeople will fold here. They had a great presentation and have associated the end user as a friend. They want to leave on a high note so they neglect to ask for the business for fear that they will disrupt this friendship they worked so hard to get. The salesperson feels confidence in their bond with the home owner that they simply pack up and ask them to call them when they are ready. I call these types "Skinny Salespeople". You worked hard to convince the home owner that you are the right person for the job. Don't do them a disservice by depriving them of the opportunity to actually buy your product. Be the hero to your customer and your boss. Question: How nice is that feeling when you go into work the next day with a signed contract? This chapter will explain how to cover objections before they become objections and close throughout the sale. I will give you all the tools the pros use to pull off the one day close. I will also explain how and why you leave cushion in the price and the reasons behind explaining post sale action steps to the end user.

Peter: Let's move on. So you did the measuring. What's next? You go back to the kitchen table and draw up the bid? What do you do next there, Jason?

Jason: At this point you can't be afraid to draw up the price. But before you do so, you want to ask them a couple questions to make sure you've closed all the hatches.

"I'm working up the numbers here. But before I give you the prices, do we look like the kind of company you'd like to do business with?" (you let them just answer them one by one). "Yeah, you're definitely a good company."

"Does this look like the kind of product you'd like to see on your house? Or do we need to explore something else?"

"Oh, yeah. We definitely want to have that product."

"Now that we've covered that we're the right company, and that this is the right product, the only left is price, right?" And you're asking questions that you're getting a 'yes' answer to. It's all yes, it's all positive, it's all head nodding. And everything is giving you that psychology, that direction towards getting the sale done.

Then it really just comes down to price. "So let me ask you, Mr. and Mrs. Smith, if I can give you a price that's reasonable and feasible, and fits within your budget, do you think this is something we can get together on today while I'm here?" And then you shut up. You have to be quiet – you can't say a word, because we all know the first person who talks loses.

But then they're going to give you one of two responses. Either they're going to say "Yeah, we can do this today." Or "No." They're going to give you an objection.

Now, if they give you an objection there's something you've missed. There's some piece of the process you didn't follow, because at this point there should be no objections because you've covered them the whole way through the process.

If they're still harping on "I'd like to see another estimate," well, just know that first objection is not the true objection. True, they want to see another estimate. But why do they want to see the other estimate? Because they want to get other prices, and that's the reality of it.

If they say they want to get other estimates, now you're at a point where you're starting to get into defense again. Now you have to rehash the whole process and everything you just went through. You've got to go back and see where you missed your step with them at the table, and that's very difficult to do.

Unfortunately, if you don't get the 'yes,' it's just about price. "There's really no reason we shouldn't be able to get together on this today." If they gave you

	an objection, then you've got to go back and cover it, and that's where it becomes a little tricky.
Peter:	Jason, I've seen this happen – and I actually did this too in my younger days when I was learning how to sell – where did the salesperson miss the step if the prospective customer says, "Well, I don't make decisions on just one bid, so I'm going to wait until I get can get a couple more"? Where did they miss the step in the sales process? What should they have brought up previous to that?
Jason:	It might not even be a step; it might just be the fact that the salesperson who was in the home wasn't keying in on the hot button. They may have covered it, but they may have gotten lost because they weren't keeping the excitement level high enough. They didn't bring them to that buying process. They stayed and thought through the process, so it could be any number of things. I can't really say where that step was missed, but something was missed.
Peter:	As far as what we call "price juxtaposition," which is comparing your price. I always used to tell my sales guys and my general managers "Be the highest or the lowest. We will always be in that upper middle" because there's a psychology to that.

As it relates to price, do you feel the same way? Why do you price yourself the way you do?

Jason: Anybody who's in the business for any extended period of time will get a handle on their competition, their pricing and structures, and what they offer (or at least you should). So when you reference a third party (like the Better Business Bureau), and you take it off yourself, now it's not you selling – it's the Better Business Bureau. It comes from a reliable source that customer can relate to that they find credible.

So when you say, "The Better Business Bureau says that if you're going to get three estimates a general rule of thumb is to go with the guy in the middle. Here's why..." and then you explain it to them.

"You've got the guy who works out of his truck. He's going to be here today and gone tomorrow. You're going to have a warranty call, a hailstorm damage, or something comes through two years later and they're not here to help you. You don't want that. That's going to be the guy who's going to be cheap because he doesn't have overhead. He's just trying to get the deal today and he's going to be gone tomorrow. You don't want to deal with those.

"Then you're going to get the other guys who have a 25-person sales force team; they're a $50 million company and they've been in it for years. But their overhead is so high that they have to charge you ridiculous margins to cover their costs. And you don't want to deal with that.

"You're getting the same product with me, and I'm going to be the guy in the middle with the price. So that's really the reality. I still give you a quality company, quality product, and quality service. And that's what you want. You want to make sure you're dealing with someone who covers all those grounds and all those bases.

"But you also want to make sure you have someone who's going to be around. My company has been in business for ten years..."
In that process you let them know upfront when you're talking about your company, "My company has been around this long. I'm not going anywhere. But I'm also not going to charge you too much either to get the product you want to put on your house."

Peter: Do you have any way to show them that? Other than verbiage, do you show them for this kind of insulated siding you're putting on, here's kind of where we sit in the industry around the local area for price. Do you have a sheet to show them? What do you do there?

Jason: You could say, "We had Mr. and Mrs. Seeley over here in this neighborhood, which is adjacent to yours, with a similar style of house. And they came in at $13,000." This is what's called "price-seeding." You let them know that "...so-and-so just down the street got siding on their house. But they also had this done and this done. They came in at $17,000." So you give them an idea.

Especially if you're the first person they're seeing, they have no clue what this is going to cost. You cover that upfront and get that out of the way, so you're price-seeding to let them know that this customer came in at $17,000 for the same product you're putting on your house, so just get that out upfront.

Now they're thinking, *Oh man, this is going to be $17,000.* Now you're coming in at $14,500. *Wow, that's better than what I thought.* Because they already had it in their mind what it was going to cost, and you come in a little under that, that's price-seeding them and you keep their expectations.

If you do a good enough job in the sales process, now they're really seeing the value, product and the service. And they're thinking, *Oh man, this is going to be really high.* But then you come in lower and they're pleasantly surprised, and then they're willing to do the deal with you.

Peter: I guess there's a couple different things here. One is the assumptive close. I used to tell my guys "When you give the price, if you let them know very confidently here's the price. And by the way this is a bargain." You never come in without confidence. Because if you immediately start talking and justifying your price, you're putting yourself – like you said – in a defensive position, and it really raises some suspicions by the buyer.

Jason: I actually had a contactor come in to my house to talk about putting a really complicated metallic hollow-back backsplash up in my kitchen that my wife wanted so badly. Now, I've never done anything like that, and I didn't want to mess it up because I knew there were going to be seven outlets to cut around. It was going to be a very demanding job, so I just wanted to hire someone to do it.

He came in, and everything was great. I loved everything he had to say, and I felt very confident in him and his company. He came by the way of a referral, so I was excited to get the work done.

But then he balked. He kind of hesitated before he gave me the price. I asked him, "Well, how much?" because he wasn't getting around to it. I actually had to pull it out of him because he didn't want to give it to me because he was fearful of it.

And because of that I already knew he was going to be way higher. Because he had never set the expectation for me, I had no clue what it was going to cost. He hesitated and then gave me the price, and before I could respond he talked again. He was done. He never had a chance. I wound up doing it myself.

The reality is if he had a process and he'd done it properly, I might have done business with him because I would have expected the number.

Peter: Exactly. So like you talked about, he missed one of those crucial steps in letting you know he was going to ask for the business.

Jason: He missed a step, and he didn't assume that I was going to do the business. He didn't have a contract ready. He never presented anything to me – he just kind of threw it out there after I had to pull teeth to get it from him. And he just lost the whole sale. All the time he spent with me went out the window with that one step alone.

Peter:	I'm sure you lost a lot of trust in him because you felt like he was trying to be secretive.
	Going back to this, so you presented the price. I agree, sometimes their first objection is not the real one. So how do you get to the real objection? You're sliding the contract across the table. But what do you if there are some other objections after that first one? How do you handle that?
Jason:	You have to go through a Q&A session. You have to start asking them questions to get to the root of it. Is it this? Is it that? If they tell you, "I'm getting other estimates," you've got to ask them, "Why are you getting other estimates?" "Well, I want to get other pricing."
	"Let me ask you, do you feel like I'm too high or too low? Are you not happy with the price? Do you not believe the price I gave you is the value that would be associated with the products and services I'm providing?"
	So you start drilling questions until you get to the root of it. And if it becomes a price issue say, "We've eliminated everything else. This is the right company. This is the right product. So the reality is the reason you want to get other estimates is because of price, right?" And you do the head "yes"

nodding, and they're saying "Yes" back to you.

You still keep that going because there's still the psychology going. You say, "You think my price is too high, and I can understand – you've never seen a price for a product like this before. Just so you know, like I said if you get two other estimates you're going to have a guy who's higher than me, and you're going to have a guy who's lower than me. I'm not going to be the low guy. I'm not going to be the high guy either. But I will be here for you, and I will help you with your service. And I can assure you, Mr. and Mrs. Smith, that this is a good price for what I'm offering you. However, there are some things I can do for you."

From a salesperson's perspective say, "I'm as low as I can get right now. I just want your business, and I'd like to go ahead and get this done today while I'm here. If you don't mind, I'm going to go ahead and make a phone call to my boss, because I can't make the decision beyond this but maybe he can help us out. Let me just give him a quick call."

So then you make the boss call. The boss understands that you're going to call him in situations like that (or at least he should understand that). And you better have something in there. Because if you're rock-bottom – if you can't go any further – that call is useless. So the only thing to take out now is your commission.

But if you have a little bit of padding in there, now you can go back and say, "This is what he's willing to do. He can get us to here."

You've got to be stern with them at this point, and you've got to be willing to say, "This is as low as I can go, but you've got to give us the business today; otherwise, this $1,000 [or $1,500] off this contract is just not going to exist if you start having other estimates come into the home. And I think you'll realize that the price as it is is really good, but you're never going to see anything like this drop." Something to that effect.

At this point you've got to be firm, and they just need to be reassured. They want to keep you honest, but you've got to keep them honest too.

Peter: Just to recap, Jason, so we really understand what you're talking about. I guess as the salesperson you should talk to the boss to know what the margins are to see if there's any extra margins. So it would make sense to call the boss where you can make an adjustment, correct?

Jason: Right. Because if you give them a rock-bottom price, the customer always wants to get a little extra – they always do.

Peter: I was going to bring that up. So the psychology there, what's going on in their mind? As an expert salesperson, why do you set that up so that they can get a little bit more? What's going on in the customer's head?

Jason: They want to feel like they're getting a better deal than anybody else; that they're actually getting a little victory in this; and that now it's an offer they can't pass up because they've worked to get a little bit more out of you. So you give them that. Don't deny them the satisfaction of hey, they got a really good deal here.

There are a lot of different ways to do it. But if you put a little bit in there so that you can take it off. Everybody has a certain margin that they have to hit, so you've got to be willing to price it maybe a little bit higher than what the reality of the cost is so that you can take it out later. Because almost always in this business that customer is going to want something off that – they're going to want more.

Also be mindful of any deals you have out there, like if you have specials going on in print marketing right now that you're not aware of, because you can get hurt. Because when it's all said and done and you've dropped a price on them, then that's when they drop a coupon on you. So you want to make sure you can cover all of that.

Peter: As we all know – just like you and I Jason – the prospective clients out there are a very educated bunch now and they do research. We have a thing called the Internet now plus all these coupon deals. So I agree with you, you've got be aware of all of that.

That psychology of getting a better deal, people love to get that because they love to tell their friends, "Guess what, I got the best deal!" This is because we've had years and years of training in the retail environment that translates over to the home services environment where people will go shopping. And how many times have you heard this when your spouse came home, "Well, I got it because it was on sale," right? We are so conditioned.

In the retail industry we all know they're running discounts for everything all the time. There's always a sale going on. So people are always shopping for a good deal because the retail industry has trained people psychologically to do that. So don't try to buck the trend with what they're already being conditioned to do like lab rats; you've got to go with that.

So I like calling the boss to be able to give them a good deal so they feel like, *You know what? I was able to bargain this guy down a little bit more, and I got the better hand of it.*

Jason: Correct.

Peter: That's very powerful. You've got the price all taken care of, so now you're going to slide the contract across the table? What happens next?

Jason: You're going to ask for their business just like you said you would. At the very beginning you told them that at the end you're going to ask for their business.

So you're just going to say, "Right here is where I need your signature," and then you just slide the contract across the table. You put it right in front of them so they have no choice but to pick up the pen. To stop you from penetrating their body with that contract they're going to grab it and they're going to look down and they're going to see the "X" and they're going to know that, *Hey, this is natural. This is what everybody does. He's comfortable enough. He's assuming I'm going to sign this contract because everybody signs the contract with this guy. I'm ready to move forward and go ahead and do business.*

Peter: If you're reading the book or doing the video course, one of the things Jason said that's so powerful is you literally draw an "X" on the signature spot where they're supposed to sign. I've seen that happen in all kinds of industries, especially in the auto dealership industry who are masters at putting the "X" down. "Sign here... sign here... sign here." This is very powerful psychology, which is by putting the "X" down you're making the assumption that they're going to sign it and that's powerful stuff that goes inside their head.

Jason: Correct.

One Day Workshops & Online Courses

As the owner of a remodeling business, have you ever wondered...
- Why is it so hard to find good salespeople?
- How do I retain good salespeople?
- How do I get out of working in my business to working on my business?
- How can I increase my sales numbers through my team?
- How can I get my team's closing ratio up?
- Is there a process that can be duplicated?
- How can I get my sales team to get the deal on the first visit?
- How can I get an edge over my competition?
- How can my team pick up some leads on their own?

What if you could...
- Hire and keep good salespeople
- Free time up for yourself and put energy into your business
- Put more money towards your bottom line
- Get a greater return on investment with your marketing dollars
- Strike fear in the hearts of your competition!

Remember when selling in the home used to be fun? What happened? Why are business owners working so hard just to keep the lights on? The One Day Close was created, field tested and mastered to bring back a selling process that has been lost over the years of a down economy. It's time to make money at this thing again. In fact, it's time your company has a break-out year. With The One Day Close system, you can do just that.

www.theonedayclose.com   **(717)292-8686**

Chapter 4: Tips and Techniques

"Tips and Techniques" This chapter offers a few secrets that will yield a long and prosperous future in sales. Successful people aren't just lucky; they are successful because they do the extras. They do the things that others don't do or aren't willing to do. A lot of salespeople need to find boldness in their approach. Don't be afraid to think outside the box. Be creative and learn how to capture more business for yourself. This chapter reveals the very things I did in my years as a successful in home salesman that not only solidified my current customer but opened the door for procuring future business.

Peter: Now they've signed. What next? You jump up and down and celebrate?

Jason: After they sign it you pack up and jump out. No, I'm just kidding. After they sign it you want to pack everything up and push it aside. You don't want to be talking business anymore.

You've got to get off-topic and cool down, because you've stuck them to the ceiling. They're excited, they're stuck on the ceiling. If you walk right out after you get that business they're going to fall down and break their bones when they hit the floor. They're scratching their heads going, *Why did we just do business with this guy? He just got a contract and left*. Now they're going to start second-guessing.

But if you stay engaged and show them that you really are interested in them beyond just this business, now you're going to have a relationship with them. So you're going to sit down and cool off, and you've got to "float them down off the ceiling" is what I call it.

You're going to float them down off the ceiling and get them back in their chairs. You're going to cool down and get off-topic – whatever it takes to not talk about business for a little while-- and make them they feel like they made a good decision. That *this is a good guy, and he truly does care about us.* It's all about the psychology of it.

Peter: One of the things I always used to do – and maybe you do this too – is I call it "future pacing." Once I got the signed contract I'd walk them through and say, "Here's what's going to happen on your project. We're so excited you're working with us. But I want to let you know kind of here's how we work and what's going to happen the first day and the second day." Do you do "future pacing" with them at this particular time?

Jason: Exactly. As you've gone through that sales process before you got them to sign, a lot of that was kind of covered. But anything that wasn't covered you want to do a recap with them. "Just so you know, Mr. and Mrs. Smith, we're about two weeks out. I have to order the product, and then it's going to be dropped into your driveway. Would you rather it be on your driveway? Or would you want it in your yard? Are you okay with that?"

"We'd like it in the driveway."

"Just so you know, if it gets dropped in your driveway, when we call you for the drop we're going to have to make sure it's clear so that we have a good place to put it. So you're going to have to keep your vehicles away from that space."

Just let them know that you're taking care of all the details. You're running them through things they never thought about. All they thought about was purchasing siding; they weren't thinking about the process.

So now you're walking them through that process. "So we're going to drop it into the driveway? Okay, great. After that I'm going to have a crew of three people who are going to come to the job. The first thing they're going to do is they're going to tear off your siding..."

You just step them through that whole thing. "When this job is complete and you're satisfied, then that's when I'm going to come back to you. You're going to see me again. I'm going to walk through this process too. I'm going to be on-sight, and I'm going to answer any questions you might have during the process of the install because I don't want there to be any surprises. If you have any issues with the installers, just give me a call.

"Some of these guys smoke, but they won't be throwing cigarette butts. They'll keep a clean workspace. They'll field dress it and throw their cigarette butts in their pouches. These guys work for me, and you're going to have a clean job site. And when we leave nothing is going to be on the ground. Everything is going to be picked up and it's going to be beautiful."

So you walk them through that process. "When it's all done, if you're completely satisfied and happy – which I'm sure you will be – the only thing I'll ask from you is would you be so kind to write me a referral letter?"

Peter: All of that stuff you just said is very powerful. It's the same process that goes on in the mind where you told them "I'm going to be asking you for the business at the end of this." Future pacing tells them here's what you're going to expect, and here's what I'm going to be doing and how I'm going to be plugged in. Then I'm going to asking you for a referral at the end hopefully if you love the job that we do. So you set that next expectation of what it is you're going to be asking them to do.

Jason: Correct.

Peter: That's very powerful. One last thing I want to bring up that Jason's talking about is bringing them off the ceiling, especially for larger scale purchases like these in home services where there are a few or several thousand dollars involved.

Future pacing is very powerful because people automatically go through a mental buyer's remorse. It's like after they sign in, in their head they're going, *Ooh, maybe I shouldn't have done that. Maybe I should have waited.* So future pacing helps them to realize that it's all right. It helps deal with buyer's remorse where, like Jason said, it brings them off the ceiling so they know what to expect and things like that.

Jason, now that you've done all of that, what's the final step or steps you would go through before you jump in your car and take off?

Jason: Going back to your last comment just so you know – if you don't mind me tackling that really quick.

Peter: Sure.

How call backs kill your business!

Jason: The thing is they've given you a $15,000 commitment, and you left them with a piece of paper that says they have three days to recede. So that's why it's super important because there is a buyer's remorse. They can be super excited, but then when they come off that high, if you're not there with them holding their hand it could be bad for you.

You just want to give them confidence and expectations for the future. You want to make them feel like you're going to hold their hand through that whole process and that they're okay. It all goes back to the psychology of it.

Can you hit me with that question one more time about what you do after the contract?

Peter: Now that you've gone through buyer's remorse, and you've done future pacing with them, are there any last and final steps before you excuse yourself and say goodbye? Is there anything you do?

Jason: I'm not sure what your angle is.

Peter: You walked them through and say here's what's going to happen. You pack up your stuff. Then is it just "Hey, thank you for your business. We will be out here at this particular time. Or you'll be getting from my office to schedule your siding." What are the final steps?

Jason: You're going to pack up your stuff. You're leave them with any applicable literature and copies of their paperwork. In a lot of cases it's best if you have a nice neat folder with your business card in it, and make sure that they keep it filed away somewhere.

And let them know, "Don't lose this. This is everything that goes on with this deal. And when this is all done I'll be adding to that. I'll be putting your warranty into this packet, so make sure you have this somewhere safe."

Smile, shake their hands, and say, "Thank you very much. Within the next one or two business days you'll be hearing from my office so that we can go ahead and stage the work to be done. And you'll be hearing from me as well throughout the process."
Then you leave.

Peter: Good. One thing I do want to touch on that you just mentioned that's really important is within one or two days your office is going to call to schedule that appointment. That's critical because you have that three-day buyer rescission, right?

Jason: Correct. Right.

How call backs kill your business!

Peter: Jason, that's another final commitment in moving forward, so maybe you can discuss that.

Jason: They do have three-day right of rescission, so you want to make sure you stay in touch with them before that period is up and keep the process moving. You don't let three days go by and not talk to them, because they will ultimately cancel. So you want to make sure you let them know "I made good on my word. I told you I was going to hold your hand through this process. I told you someone was going to reach out to you."

This furthers the commitment and solidifies their thoughts and their confidence in you and your company that this guy's been true, they've done everything they said they were going to do. They called me, there's no need to cancel. Let's move forward.

Another good thing to do is to plant a sign out in their front yard so it gives them a reminder. That's another commitment. Before I write the final number on the contract I ask, "You know what, I have a yard sign. Would you be okay if I took $100 of this and plant a sign in your yard?" They'll go, "Oh, yeah. Sure."

Inevitably what almost always happens is they'll say, "You can plant ten signs in my yard." That's another win for them. *Oh, I'm getting another $100 off. Yeah, let's do it!*

Then you take Mrs. Smith outside and say, "Hey, Mrs. Smith, where would you like me to put this?" Now they get to place the sign and that's a big deal. So you don't just randomly pick a spot – you let them pick the spot.

Peter: Are you putting the yard sign in right there before you leave after you sign the contract? Or do you do that later?

Jason: I do. I do realize that sets yourself up for other predators to go around and see signs and call on that customer. You'll get that from time-to-time. But I don't have any fear of losing business to those guys who are willing to do that.

I plant the sign right away because I want referrals to start generating off that immediately. And then I let them know, "If we get this thing in here, anybody who calls as a referral off this sign is going to be more money to you. I'll give you $50 for every person who calls me as a result of the sign in your yard. And all they have to do is set an appointment with me."

Peter: Exactly. That is so powerful. I want to make sure, guys, that you understand the steps Jason is doing. Number one, by planting that sign and letting the customer decide where they want it put out in their front yard, they're getting another win and another small commitment because you're giving them $100 off.

Number two, they're getting to choose where they want to put it.

Number three, Jason is getting the sign up before he leaves which is very important for step four.

Jason, you talked about pamphleting the neighbors. When you go out to the neighbors I'm assuming you're doing that before you leave, right? You go up to the door, knock on it and give them the pamphlet and say what you said here in the book. "Look across the street. Do you see that sign over there? That's the neighbor I'm doing the work for." Is that what you do?

Jason: Yeah, that's exactly what I do. There are all kinds of nice tips and tricks and things that are neglected by a lot of salespeople. But if they take the time to do these things, that's money. That's marketing and it just makes sense.

It's kind of like a realtor: If they sell one house in a neighborhood, they wind up selling all the houses in the neighborhood because they all saw that one sign and that's who they know. *This person knows the area. This homeowner has confidence in this realtor so I'll call them.*

Everybody wants to keep up with the Joneses. So if they see a sign in a yard they know that neighbor's already done all the hard work, leg work and research. They've already met with the person. They've decided to do business with you over everybody else, so that eliminates all the opportunities for everybody else because they feel confident that if I call this guy, this homeowner has already done all this work and that's going to make it a little easier for me.

Peter: That's very powerful. And we talked a little bit earlier about the fact that like attracts like, and even the houses are all alike because they were typically built in the same timeframe. If one is having a siding or working issue, probably others are in the neighborhood.

This whole idea that Jason is talking about putting yard signs out and then going out to pamphlet the neighborhood before you go could mean thousands more in your pocket in commissions by doing those little things he's talking about.

Jason, now we've gone through the whole process from a first phone call all the way through to finishing up with that particular customer.

We're going to have a bonus section in this book I want to go through and we'll go into detail. You talked about some of these bonus things you do like calling the boss (we covered that and that'll be in there), dropping yard signs, and doing the pamphlet marketing.

but there are a couple other ones I want you to bring up, and then any ones that maybe I missed. You have a thing called "the special" on calling appointments. What's that all about, and how does that help the client?

Jason: When you give the customer the price, but you see they're stalling on you and they're talking about it, you can say, "I've got a special going on," because you know they have other estimates behind you.

If you've done your fact-finding, you know at this point in the game that they have other estimates coming in and you can see that's what's holding them up. *Man, how am I going to tackle these other estimates I have lined up because*

I'm doing business with this guy? I don't want to sit through this anymore.

Because you know that's what's going on in their head you let them know upfront, "I've got a special going on. Do you want to hear about it?" Of course, yeah, everybody wants to hear about a special.

Then you say, "Mr. and Mrs. Jones, I appreciate the opportunity you're giving me. And after you do business with me I want to offer you this one-time opportunity that once we sign this contract and start moving forward in our process, I'm going to personally call and cancel all the other appointments you have already." They might laugh – and a lot of times they will laugh because they think that's the funniest thing to say and it seems silly.

But you're being bold at this point, because when you have a relationship in this process you can be a little bold. You can say, "I'm curious about this. If I come out here and see another competitor's sign in your yard, I'm just going to pull over and puke right there in the yard." That's funny stuff, but it's another way to connect with them. You're starting to loosen the muscles it takes to sign a piece of paper.

Then you tell them, "I'll call and cancel because here's the reality of that. If that guy comes out here, and you already know you want to business with me and if you sign this contract, the last thing that other salesperson wants to do is come out here and waste their time on an appointment that has already going somewhere else.

"Do them a favor – because I know personally I would really appreciate it if people would cancel on me if they're doing business with somebody else – and allow them the opportunity to go have another appointment with somebody who might do business with them." They'll pause and agree that makes sense.

Then you have to make good on that. "All right. So let me go ahead and make these calls, and I'll do it right in front of you." So you call that company and let them know, "Mr. and Mrs. Jones is already doing business with somebody else. I just wanted to give you a quick courtesy call to let you know that there's no need to send a salesperson out here. You can set another appointment for them." They'll say, "Thank you for the call," or whatever, blah-blah-blah.

But you don't let them know that "I'm the salesperson for such-and-such company" because now that salesperson is going to call back and say, "I'm going to be in the area. How about if I just give you a quick estimate? I'll just measure really quick and give you a price." Then they're snaking their way back into the deal. So you want to make sure that you cancel that for them.

Now, if you leave it up to the homeowner to cancel, first off they won't make the call. Or they'll still keep the appointment. Or when they do call the salesperson on the other line is going to snake their way back in. They're going to be crafty because they are salespeople, and it's easy enough to say, "Why don't I just come out there? I'll give a quick measurement and leave you a price. I won't take up two hours of your time. I'll just leave you a price."

They already know you. They know their competition and they know their pricing, so all they've got to do is be lower. Now they're going to back in there and have an opportunity to talk, because now the homeowner wants to pay less and they want to see what they have to offer. They're going to snake their way back into the appointment, so that's why it's important for you to make the call.

Peter: Like you were saying earlier, I like the way you said you do it right there with them. By and large people don't like confrontation. You're doing the dirty work for them. You're calling the business back not as the salespeople who sold them, but just to let the other company know the deal is done.

And you're doing it in that three day right of rescission window where you could lose it. That's where you want to do it, because you want to remove that risk. Even though they signed the contract, they have three days to rescind it. So I like what you're doing there by helping them.

Again, you could almost call is buyer's remorse, but you're helping them make that commitment once again to you and your company. So that's a good tip and tactic.

Jason: They absolutely hate confrontation. They actually called to set the appointment, so they don't want to have to call and cancel it and be the bad guy. In some cases, the people on the other line can be pretty nasty back, and pretty pressing and firm, because they've got nothing to lose. So you don't want to put your customer through that experience.

Peter: Exactly. It can be very negative. That's a good one.

Let's move on to the next tip and tactic here, which is you call it "I've got to make a call." Tell us about how you excuse yourself. What's the psychology there, and why would you do that?

Jason: I love all of these. You have a customer who's on the hook. You know they're going to make that decision. Through the entire sales process you've kept these two apart -- they haven't been able to communicate once.

Now, this is a big decision. Anybody who has a husband or wife can tell you, you just don't make decisions without talking about them. Sometimes they do. Right there, boom. They've made their decision. They're good so let's move forward.

But sometimes they need just a minute to say, "Do we want to do this? Let's weigh this out." In just a minute or two you can see them kind of hesitating just because they want to have that conversation. When you read their body language you know that's all it is. At this point you have confidence they're going to do business with you.

You just need to let them have one moment of peace to be able to talk to each other without you present. And they'll even tell you, "We just need to talk about this." You say, "Great. My wife called me a couple times during our time together here. Why don't I step out to my car and call her back? I'll just wait for you to step back out and wave me back in when you're ready and when you've made a decision one way or the other. It's okay. I'm just going to go out and make this phone call to my wife. You let me know when you're ready. Is that fair enough?" They'll say, "Yeah, sure."

So you go out to your car and make that fake phone call (or you actually make a phone call, whatever). You've got to be willing to hang that thing up right away when they wave you in.

Or if it's dark outside say, "Do me a favor and turn your porch light on when you're ready for me to come back in."

Peter: Flash the Morse Code. Yeah, there you go.

Jason: It works like a charm. I've never done that and not gotten the business. Every single time I got the deal when I did that.

Peter: That's a really powerful one, and I love that because sometimes that's all they need. You've got to let the husband be the fixer and the educator, and you've got to let the wife be the decision-maker. Sometimes they're not comfortable do that in front of you.

Like you said, when you're confident that you've got the deal, be confident in that and excuse yourself and go out to the car. Call whoever. Call for dinner reservations or something, but just let them have their time. That's really good.

Jason: Many people when people say, "We need to talk about it," they'll think, *Oh, they need a few days to talk about it*, and they'll leave and call back and go back to the appointment. When the reality is all they need is one minute to have a discussion. So you just go out to your car and give them that.

Peter: Usually when they're amped up, now's a good time.

Jason: While they're on a high.

Peter: Exactly. Let's move on to the next tip and tactic you have here. You call it "The Columbo." So tell me a little bit about The Columbo.

Jason: That just goes down to when you start getting the objections. That's the whole thing we were discussing earlier about just doing back and rehashing the whole process. Everything you went through, everything they said yes to and agreed to throughout the whole presentation. So when they're giving you an objection you go back to that.

Now, everyone who knows that TV figure Columbo (at least anybody who's my age and older) understands that he had a process to let the criminal incriminate themselves. He went through a line of simple, easy, straightforward questions where the end result was there was no way out. That criminal was backed into a corner and they incriminated themselves. Somewhere they slipped because their story wasn't matching up.

It's the same thing here. You do a "Columbo" approach where you say, "Let me ask you. You said you liked our company, correct? It's the kind of company you'd like to do business with. Am I right?" "Yeah."

"Is this not the right product? This is the product you want to see on your house, right?" "Well, yeah. I'd love to have that on my house."

"Okay, good. You like me? Is it me?" So you go through all these things. "I just want to make sure I'm not missing something, because I don't want to do a disservice here. I want to make sure I've covered everything, so let's just go through this. So it's just a matter of pricing. Is that right? Is that all it is?"

"No, it's not about price."

"So it's not about price. You like the company, you like the product, and you like the price."

Then you start eliminating every possible objection for them. They're not giving it to, so you've got to find it. Once you find that objection, then you can cover it and that's what that's all about.

Peter: Jason, in that Columbo approach after you've eliminated everything, do you ever ask them, "What is it that's causing you not to make a decision today?"

Jason: At this point when you get into that and you're doing the Columbo approach, that means you're getting objections which means you missed something in your sales process. So it's okay at this point and you might as well be frank and honest. You've already torn the walls down, and you guys can be open with each other.

You can even tell them, "Hey, I just want to be open and honest with you. Let's just cut to it because I just want to figure out where's the hesitation. What is it that's catching you here?" And be honest – don't be afraid to be firm and committed to it.

At this point they've taken two hours of your time. They're not giving you everything you need to know to get the

	deal, so sometimes you've got to turn it up a notch.
Peter:	That leads me to the next technique you talk about here as it relates to this questioning process with Columbo. You call it "The Tennis Ball Technique." Can you talk a little bit about what that is?
Jason:	If you ever watch a game of tennis you see heads that are going left and right and left and right and left and right. So basically what happens is if someone gives you a question, you don't really give them an answer without returning a question to them. Like the example I have here, if they ask you "What kind of siding do you offer?" Well, that's a very general question. You can't really answer that because you might have ten different kinds of siding options for them. You don't want to start talking about one and that's not really the fit for them. So you say, "What kind of siding would you like on your house?" If they say, "Whenever I'm using the weed eater it keeps chipping up." Or "I have issues with it fading." Or "It's chalking." Then you start eliminating everything else. *I'm not going to put an 040 grade siding on their house. They're wanting something maybe a little nicer.*

	Then they start asking you other questions, and you start returning them in the same manner until you let them decide and dictate what you're going to present to them.
Peter:	So by putting the question back in their court you're allowing them to get a little more specific in their own mind about what it is they're asking you, I guess is really what this Tennis Ball Technique is about.
Jason:	Right. That's where you can kill yourself. If you don't let them get specific to you, then you can talk in generalities. Then that's when you're going to be spending way too much time in the home.
Peter:	This gets back to what you were saying earlier in the notes you sent to me. It's kind of like you have two ears and one mouth. It's better to listen more and talk less which helps.
Jason:	Exactly right.
Peter:	The Tennis Ball Technique is a good one. The other one I really like that you brought up is you have what you call "The Barbeque Technique." Tell me a little bit about your Barbeque Technique, and how that works with customers.

Jason: This is my absolute favorite one, and I don't know of anybody who has ever done it other than myself. But I've always had so much success with it. This is something I hear people saying, "Yeah, I'm going to use that." But boy, I tell you if you really do it, it truly does pay off.

You get the deal, you've chummed it up with the customer, and they're super excited. They love the work and they want to brag about it. So give them an opportunity to do that and say, "Mr. and Mrs. Smith, this is maybe going to sound like an odd request, and you probably haven't heard of anything like this before.

"But I tell you what would be really cool is would you be open to doing maybe a barbeque for your friends and family if I provide the burgers and dogs and man the grill for you? And all you've got to do is invite some friends and family and show off my work. Would you be open to that?"

"Yeah, sure. Why not?"

So the next thing you know they have a barbeque and they invite 10-12 friends and family over. They see the work that was done. And they talk you up, because why would they have you there if they wouldn't talk you up, right?

You have business cards handy, you man the grill, and you start conversing with everybody. Now all of a sudden there's one, two or maybe three people out of that whole group who need work done.

Well, they're not going to call and get estimates from anybody else because all the hard work has been done. That customer of yours knows them personally, and they know them and they know they've done all the hard work. So now they don't have to do the hard work. Now it turns into what's called a "gold lead" instead of a "cold lead."

Peter: That's really powerful. And I know this sounds kind of a goofy, but to take that even one step further you could have an apron made that has your yard sign on the front of it so they can immediately recognize you at the barbeque. "Oh, you're the siding guy." You know what I'm saying?

Jason: Right. Or something silly, like maybe a cow and a chicken on the front of it to show a little personality. And be friendly, kind and courteous.

If you do that you will get business out of it. It may not be right away, but they're going to keep your card. Down the road they may not have your card,

	but they'll say, "Who was that guy who did that barbeque for you? I've got to get some work done." And that goes a long way for you.
Peter:	It really does. That's really good. So Jason we went through a lot of your tips and techniques. We went through the whole process from front to back, and you shared all your secrets about what you do that got you to write over a million dollars in business on a consistent basis, not only for the company you worked for but your own company. In these interviews, I always wrap up with probably one of the toughest questions. I want to ask you if you had one or two things to pass on to people you've learned over the years to help you become the most successful salesperson in your company, what would that be?
Jason:	One: Get some mentorship. Find people who are successful and learn from them. Two: Don't think you're so successful that you can't learn because you can always learn. Three: When you get a little bit longer in the tooth in this business, sometimes you think you've got it so together and you're so good that you start neglecting the steps. Then you'll start seeing your business fall off.

So always follow the process from front to back. Never neglect a step because you want to hurry it up or you think you're better than that. Never go without following the entire process from beginning to end, because your sales will suffer if you don't stick to your process and make it second nature.

Peter: This is very powerful stuff, and I couldn't agree with you more. Don't cut corners. And good professional salespeople follow a process.

I liked your other tip about I used to always call it "Success leaves traces. Copy what others are doing." This is why you're reading this book.

By the way, if you really liked what you read here and you want to find out more about Jason Blevins and his other products he has to offer for people being successful in the home services sales business, you can go over to www.theonedayclose.com. He's got some good video courses there, and some other very useful tools and Things so you can really learn the value of this.

The whole idea, guys, is Jason's here as your mentor and as your advisor. And most importantly, he's here to put more money into your pocket and your bank account by helping you to up your game as a sales professional.

So with that, Jason, thank you very much for spending the time here and talking all about your whole process. This was incredible. Thank you.

Jason: Thank you very much. I appreciate the time.

How call backs kill your business!

One Day Workshops & Online Courses

As the owner of a remodeling business, have you ever wondered…
- Why is it so hard to find good salespeople?
- How do I retain good salespeople?
- How do I get out of working in my business to working on my business?
- How can I increase my sales numbers through my team?
- How can I get my team's closing ratio up?
- Is there a process that can be duplicated?
- How can I get my sales team to get the deal on the first visit?
- How can I get an edge over my competition?
- How can my team pick up some leads on their own?

What if you could…
- Hire and keep good salespeople
- Free time up for yourself and put energy into your business
- Put more money towards your bottom line
- Get a greater return on investment with your marketing dollars
- Strike fear in the hearts of your competition!

Remember when selling in the home used to be fun? What happened? Why are business owners working so hard just to keep the lights on? The One Day Close was created, field tested and mastered to bring back a selling process that has been lost over the years of a down economy. It's time to make money at this thing again. In fact, it's time your company has a break-out year. With The One Day Close system, you can do just that.

www.theonedayclose.com   (717)292-8686

Made in the USA
Middletown, DE
12 June 2016